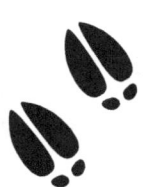

# This Coloring Book Belongs to:

I0446931

_____

Each coloring book you purchase plays a vital role in wildlife conservation and habitat preservation. We at MyTravel4Ever refer to these as 'Impact Moments'. Discover which organization benefits from your purchase by scanning the QR code. You'll receive an Impact Certificate, detailing the specific cause your purchase is helping to support. Or visit www.MyTravel4Ever.com

SCAN ME

SCAN ME

We also design unique trips centered around wildlife, photography, and adventure, and you're invited to come along! Embark on an exciting journey with us. Scan the QR code to discover what adventures we have coming up next! Or visit www.MyTravel4Ever.com/adventures

Reviews help spread the word so we can make a bigger impact. Please take a moment and tell us what you like about the coloring book by scanning the QR code!

# AFRICA

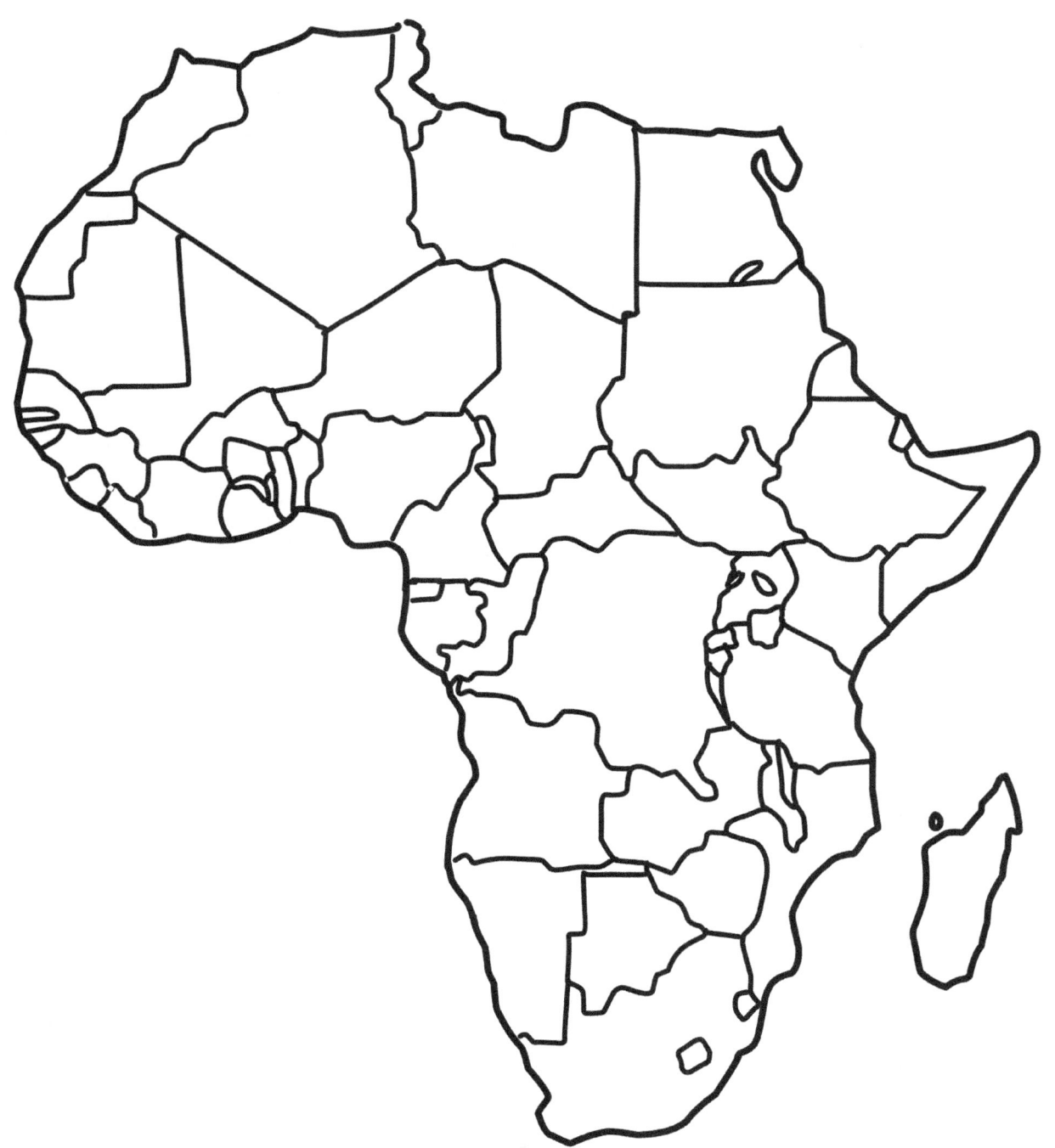

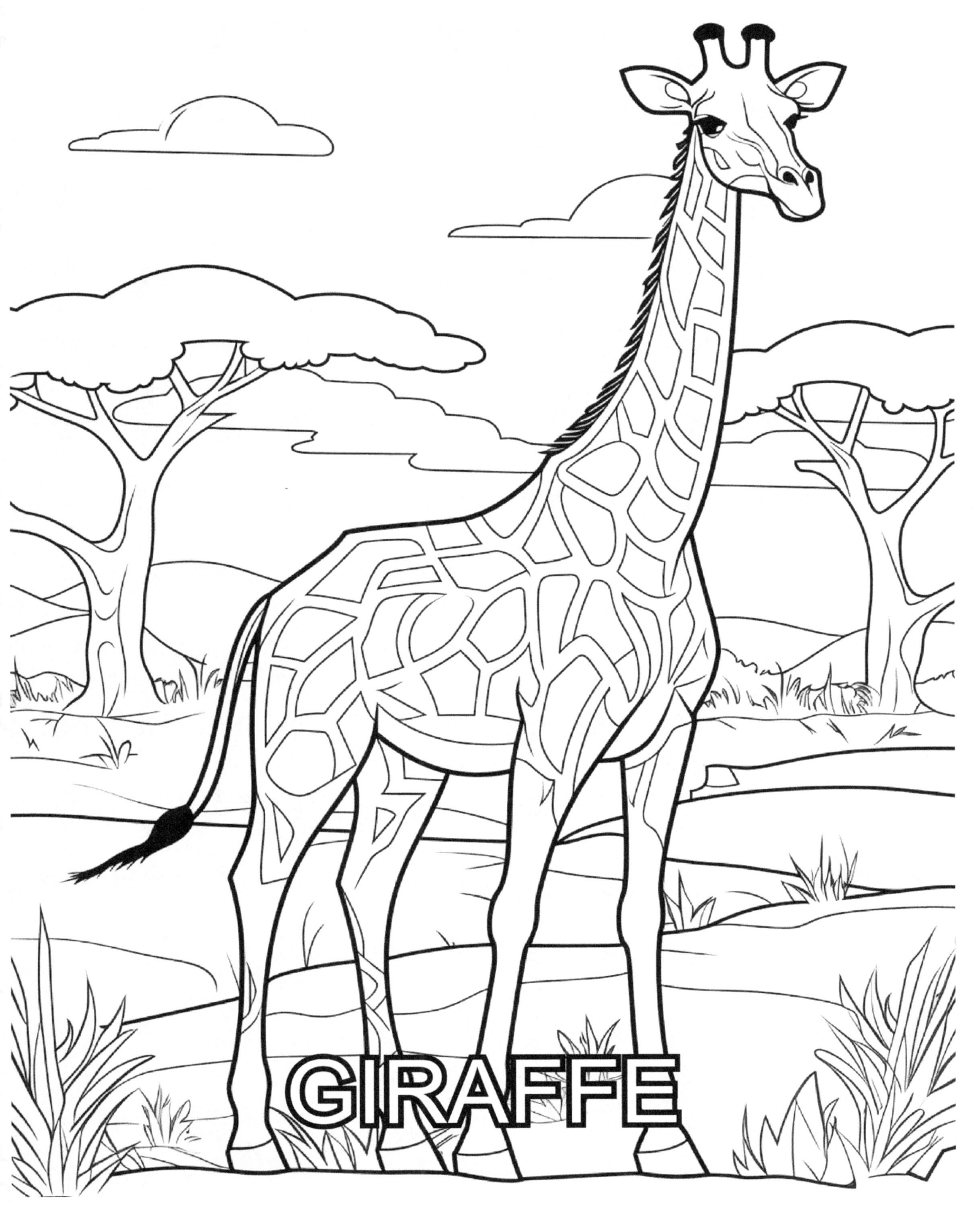

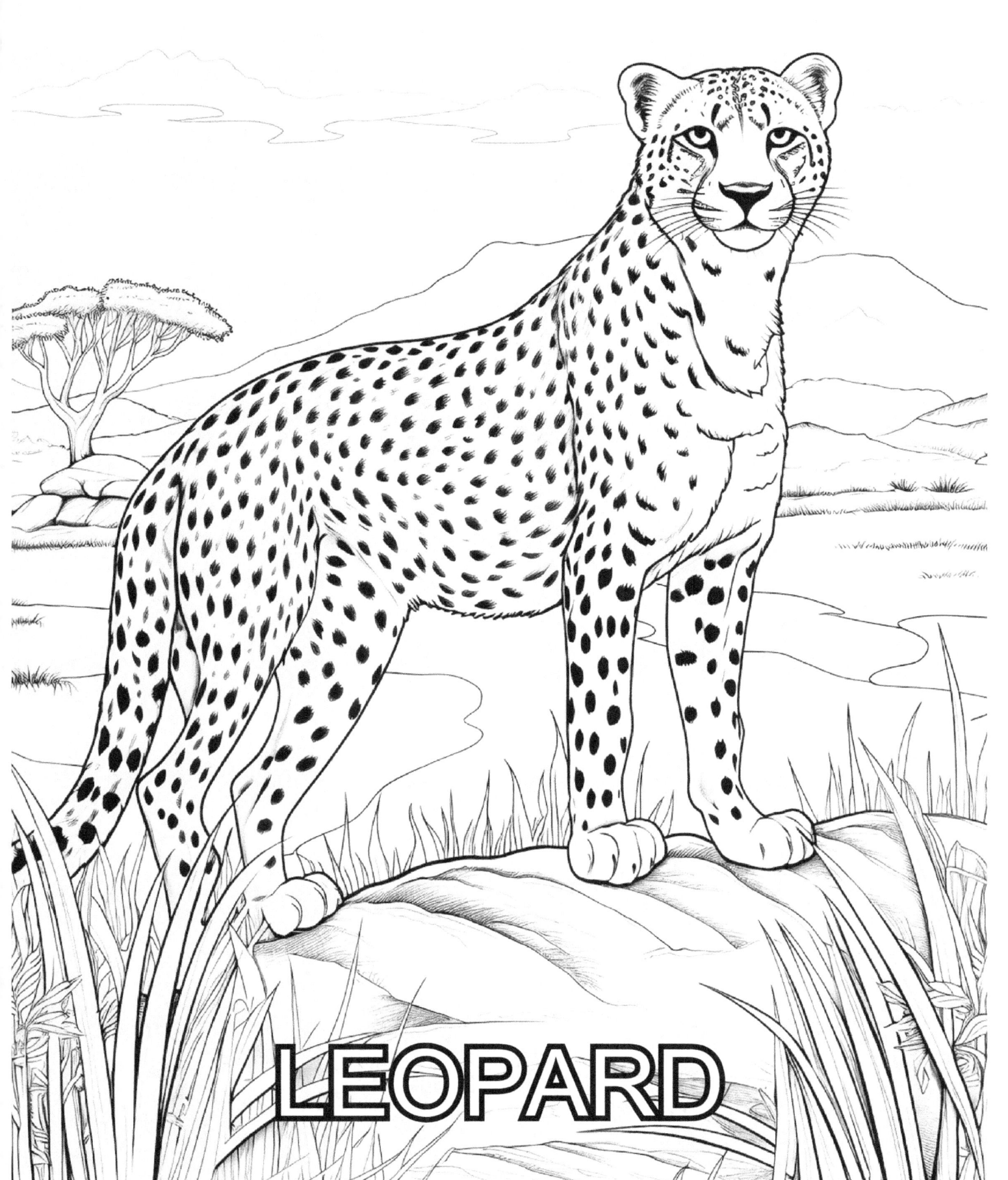

LEOPARD

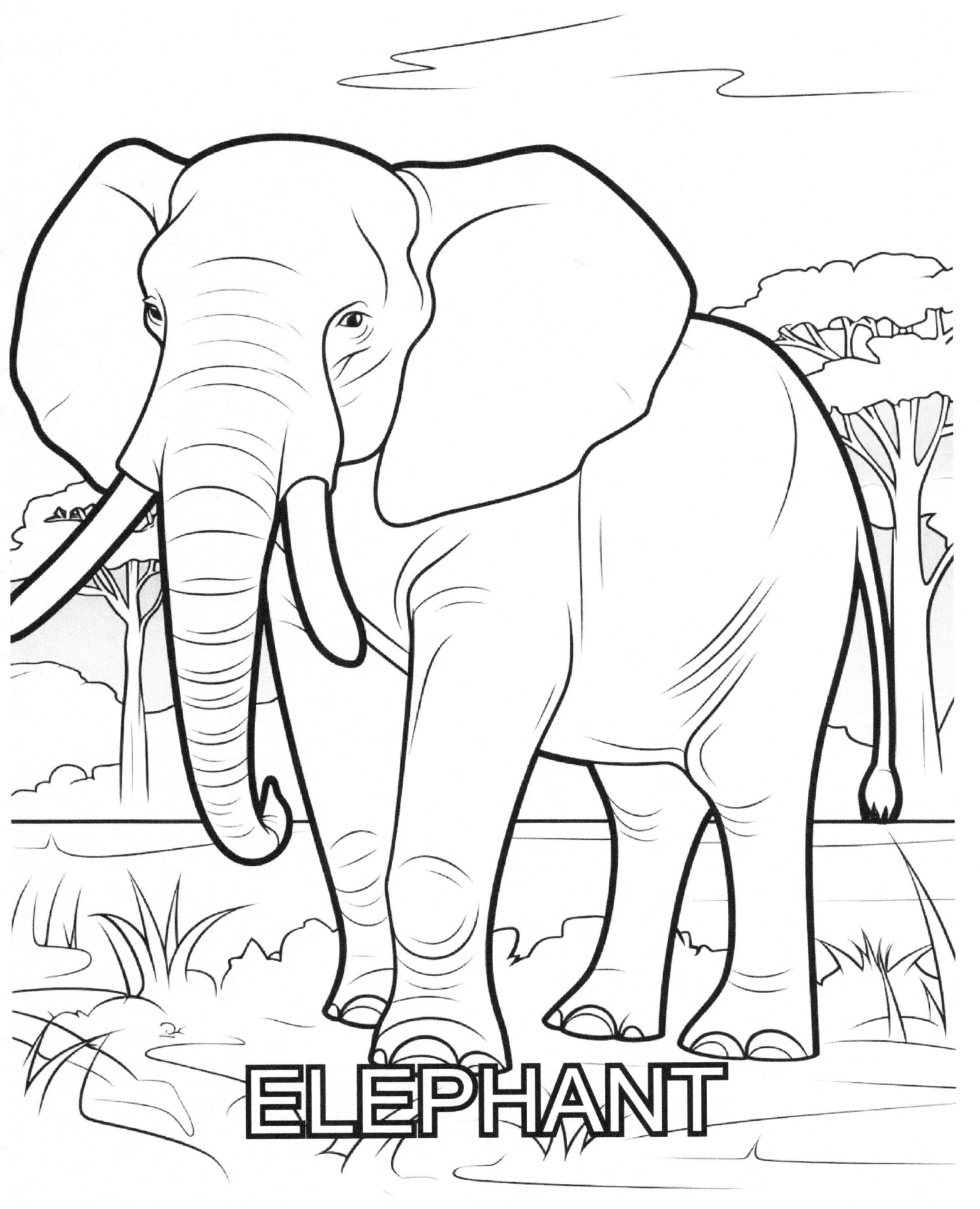

ELEPHANT

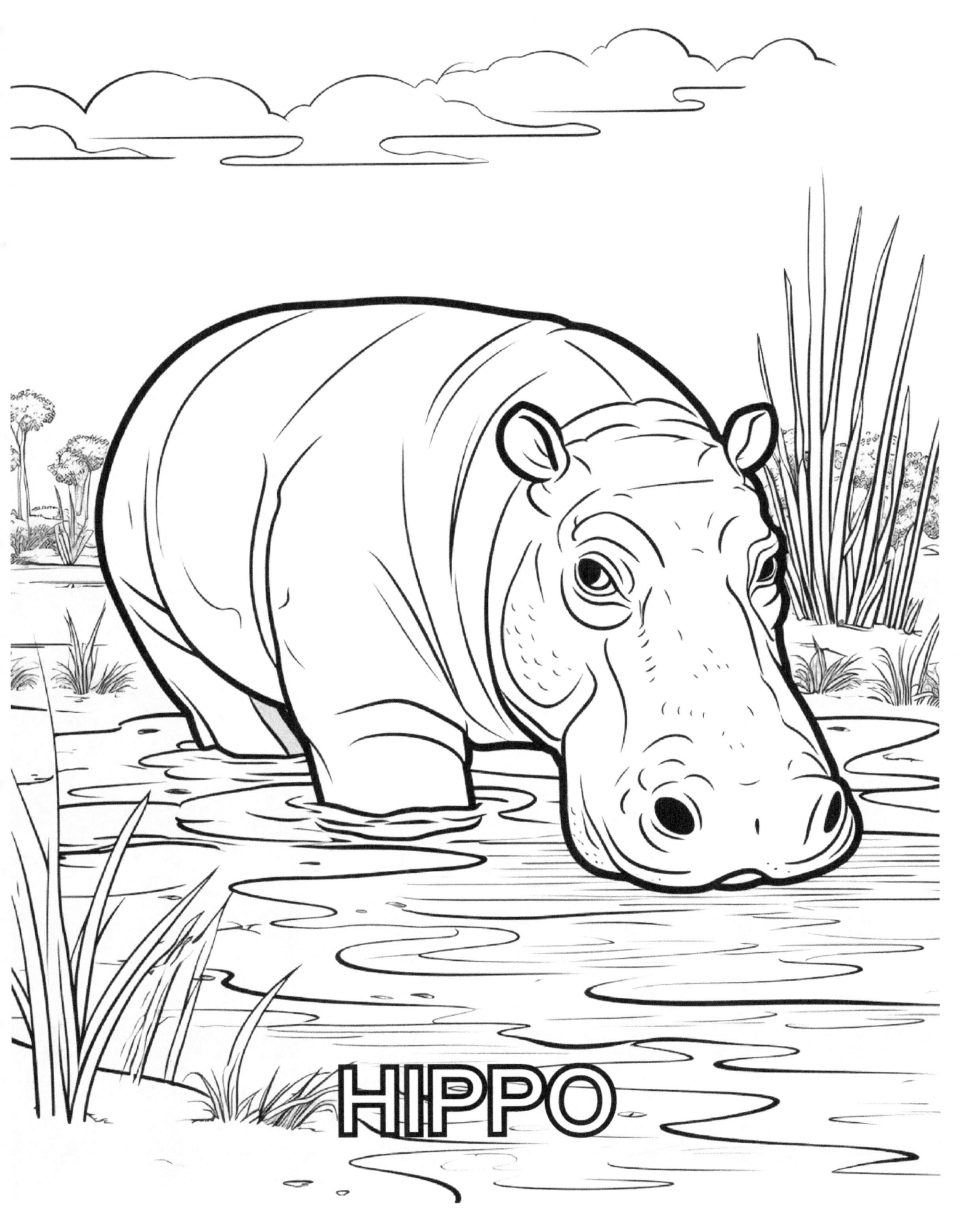

HIPPO

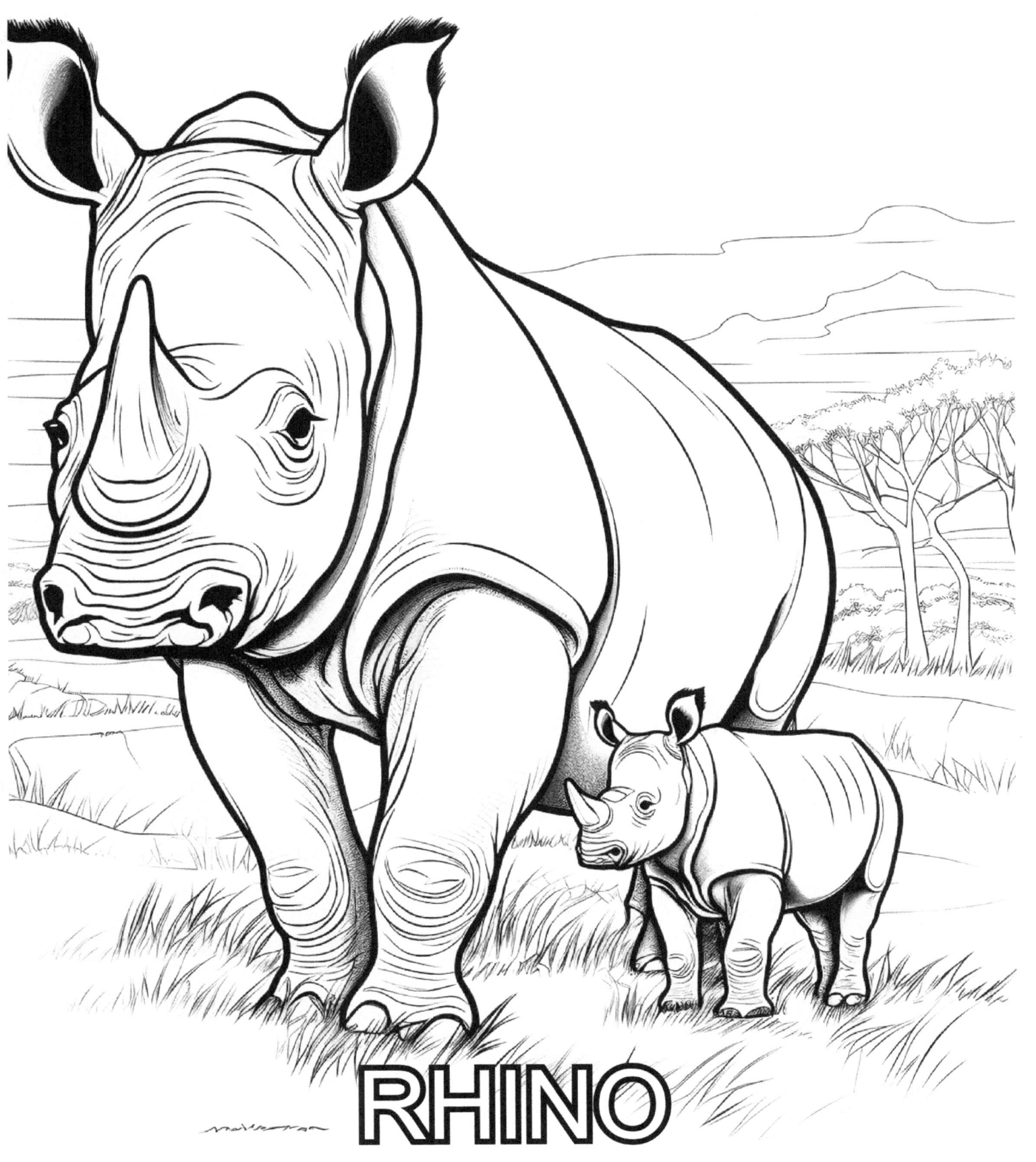

RHINO

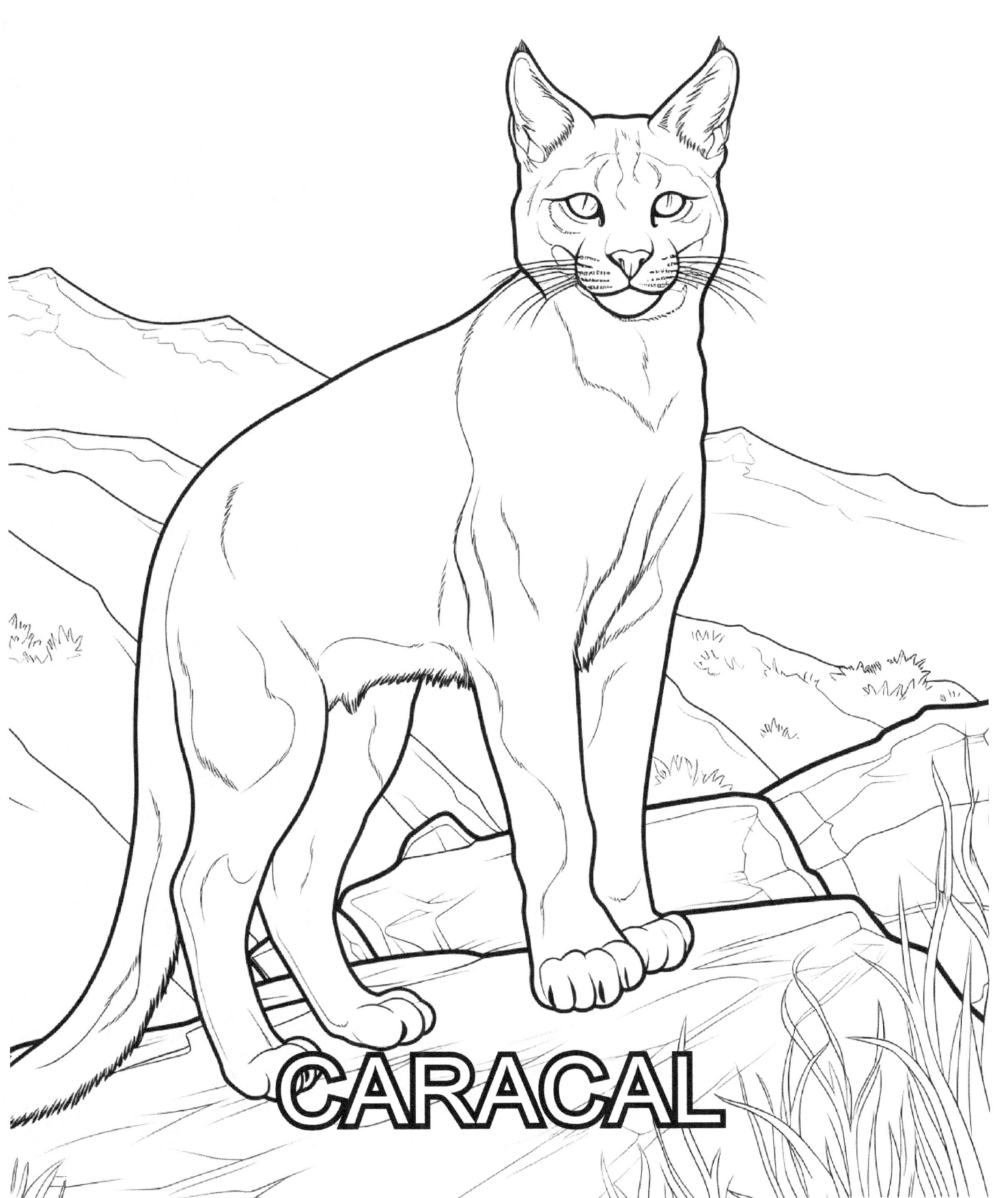
CARACAL

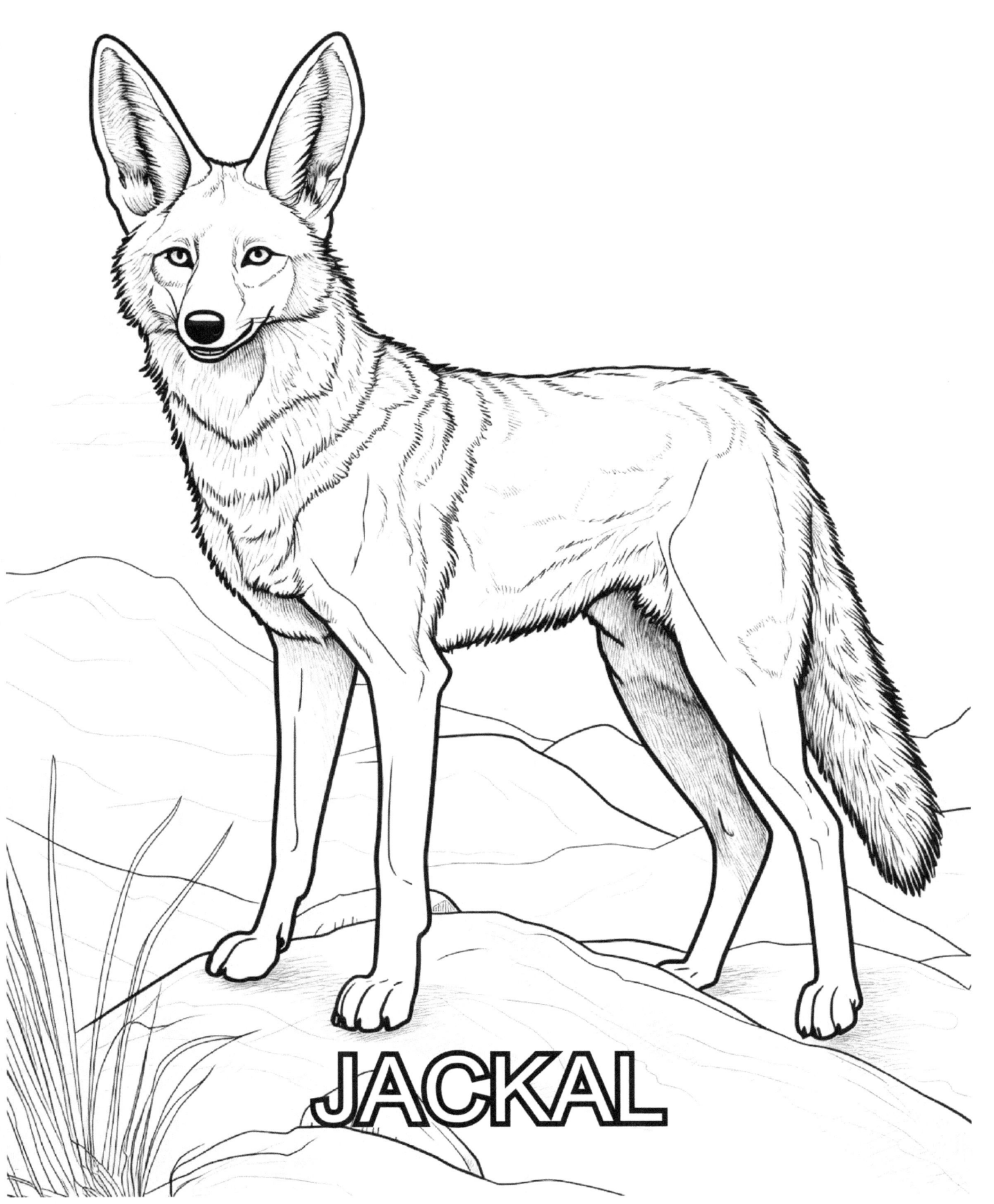

JACKAL

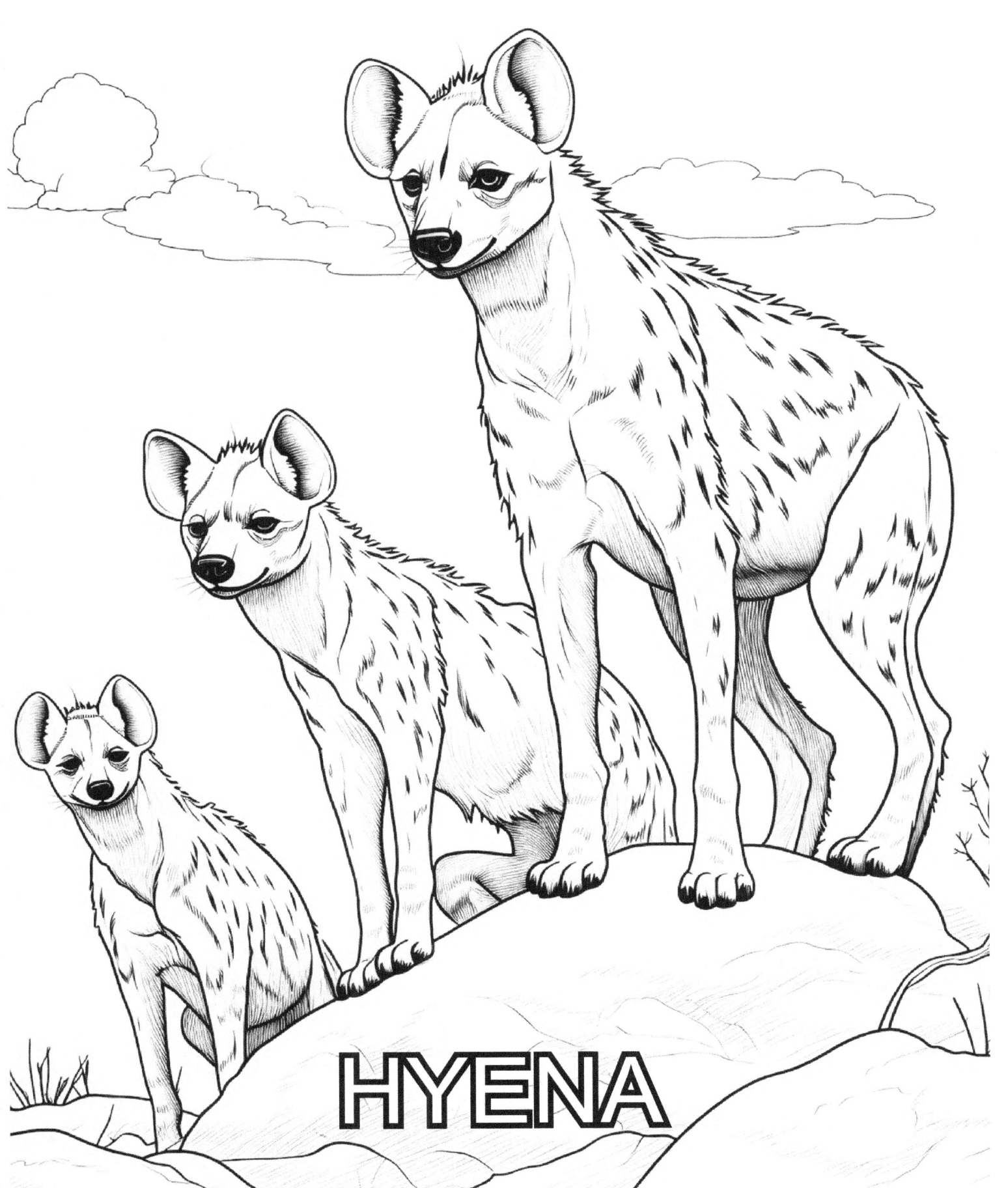

HYENA

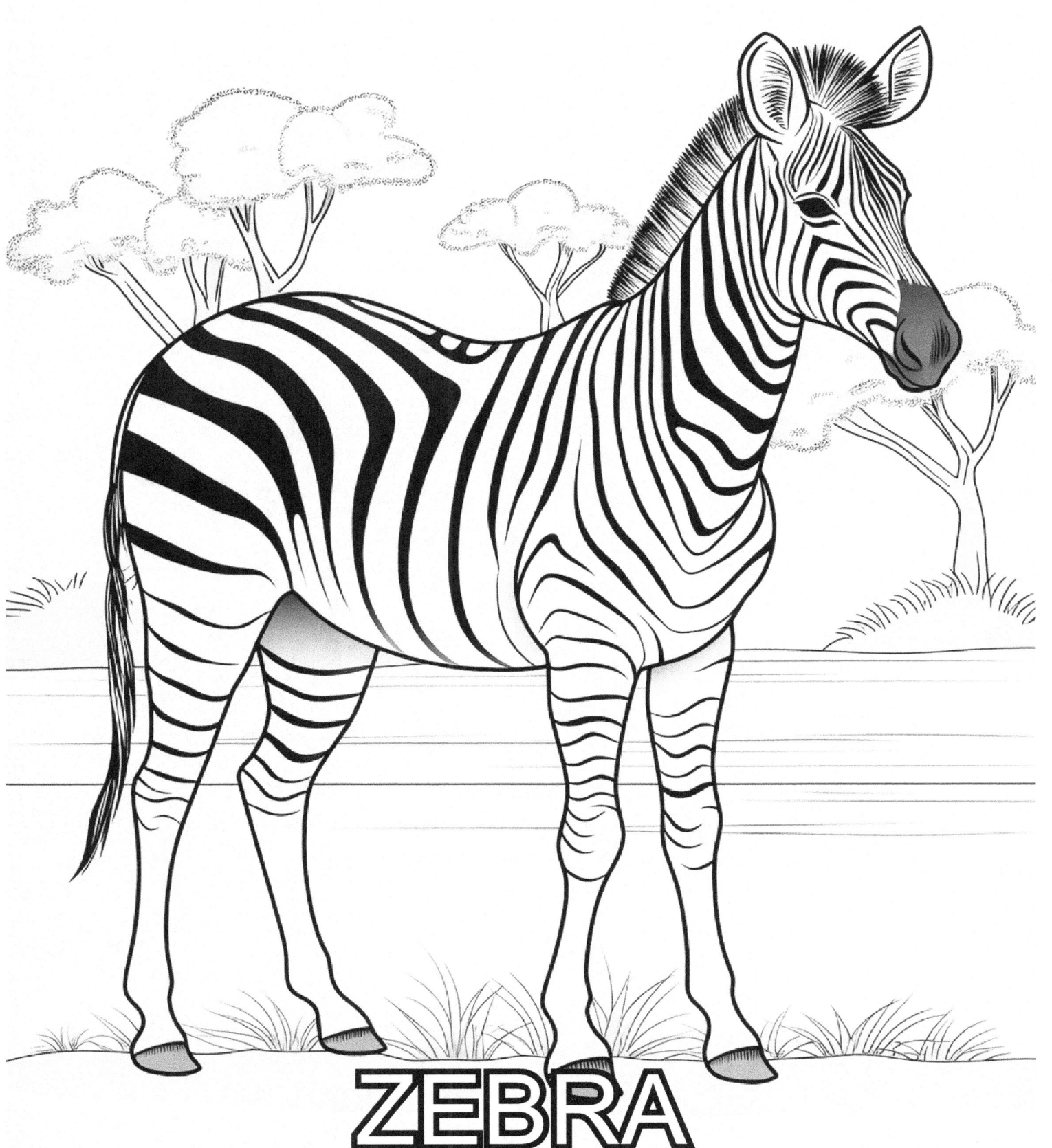

ZEBRA

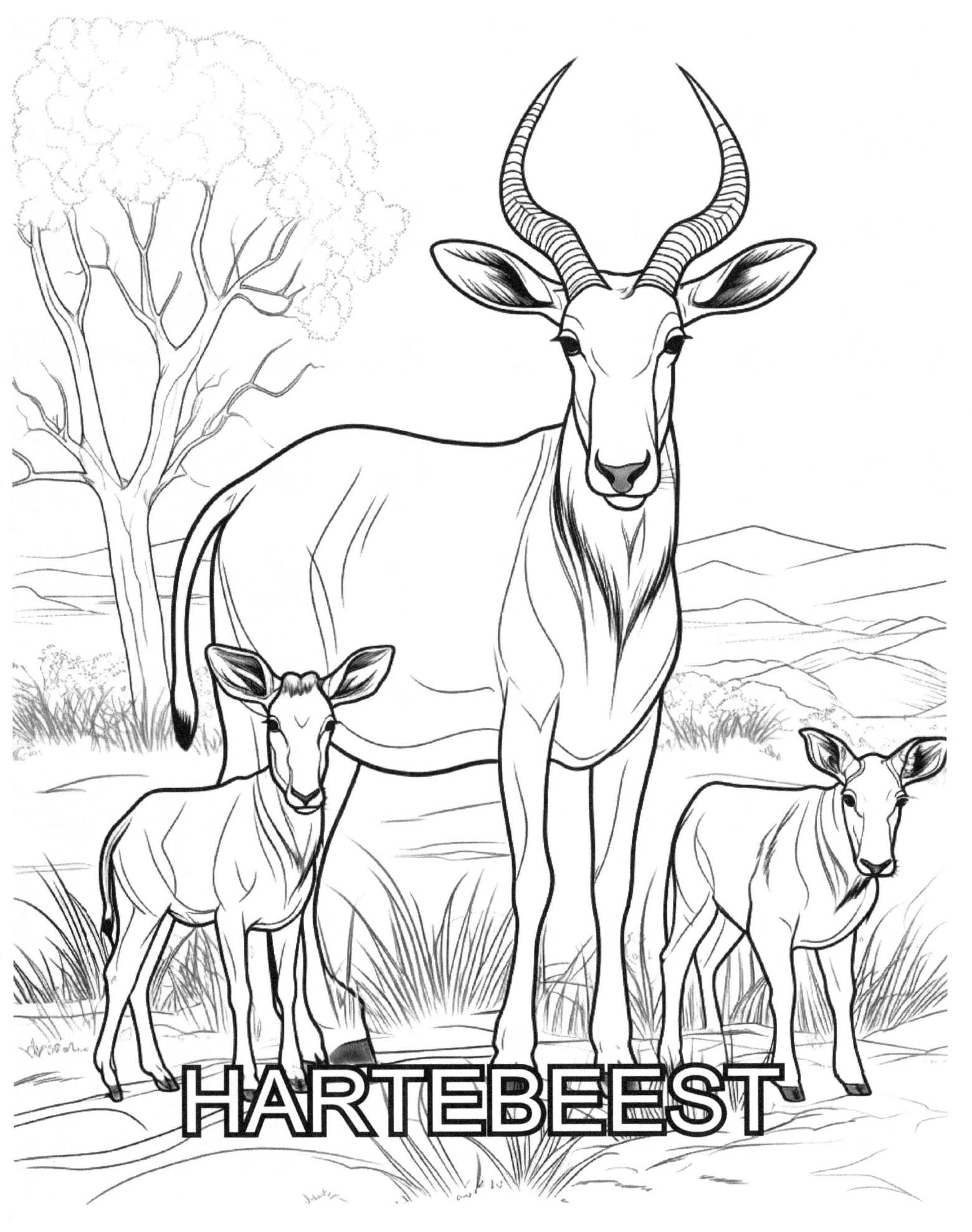

HARTEBEEST

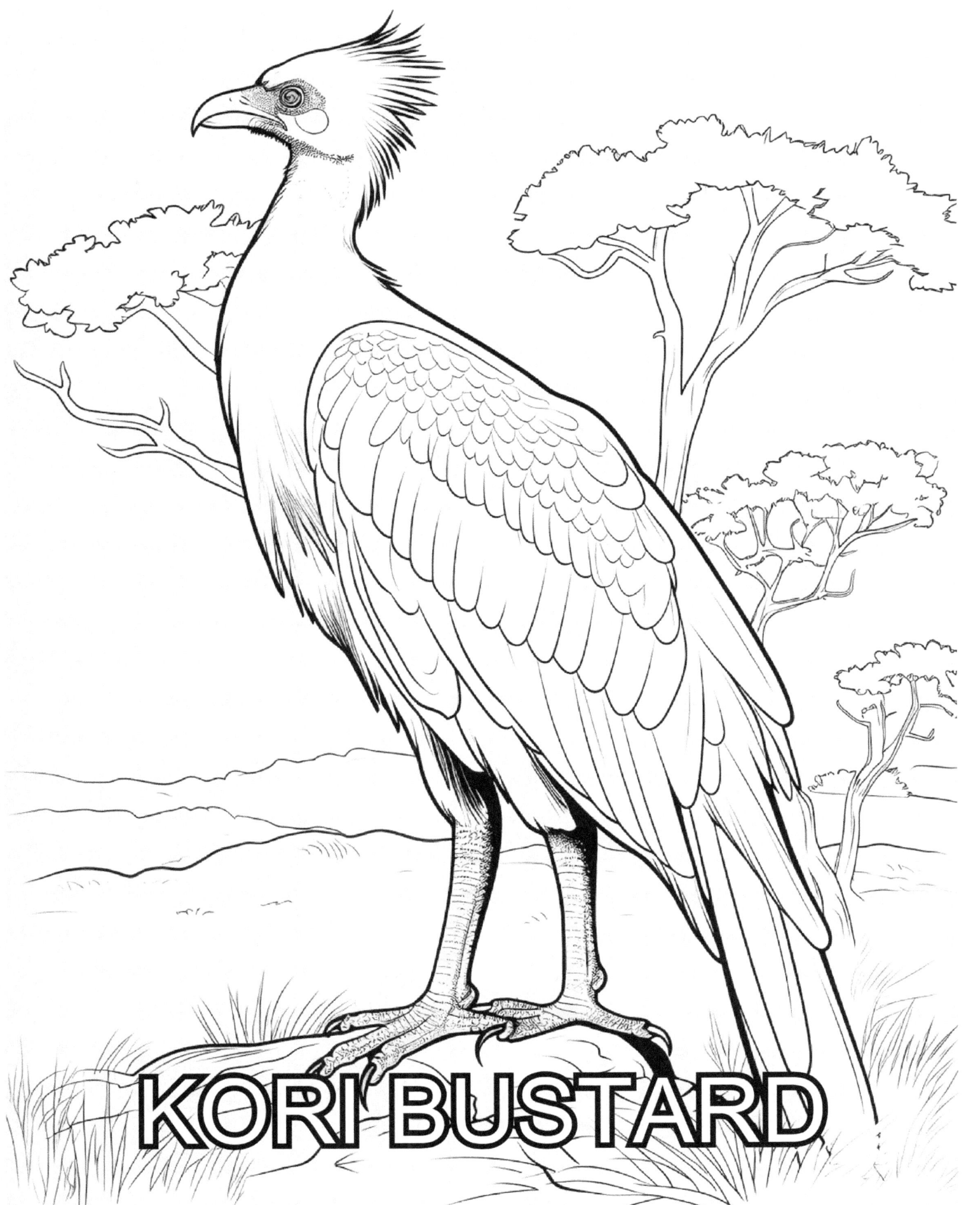

KORI BUSTARD

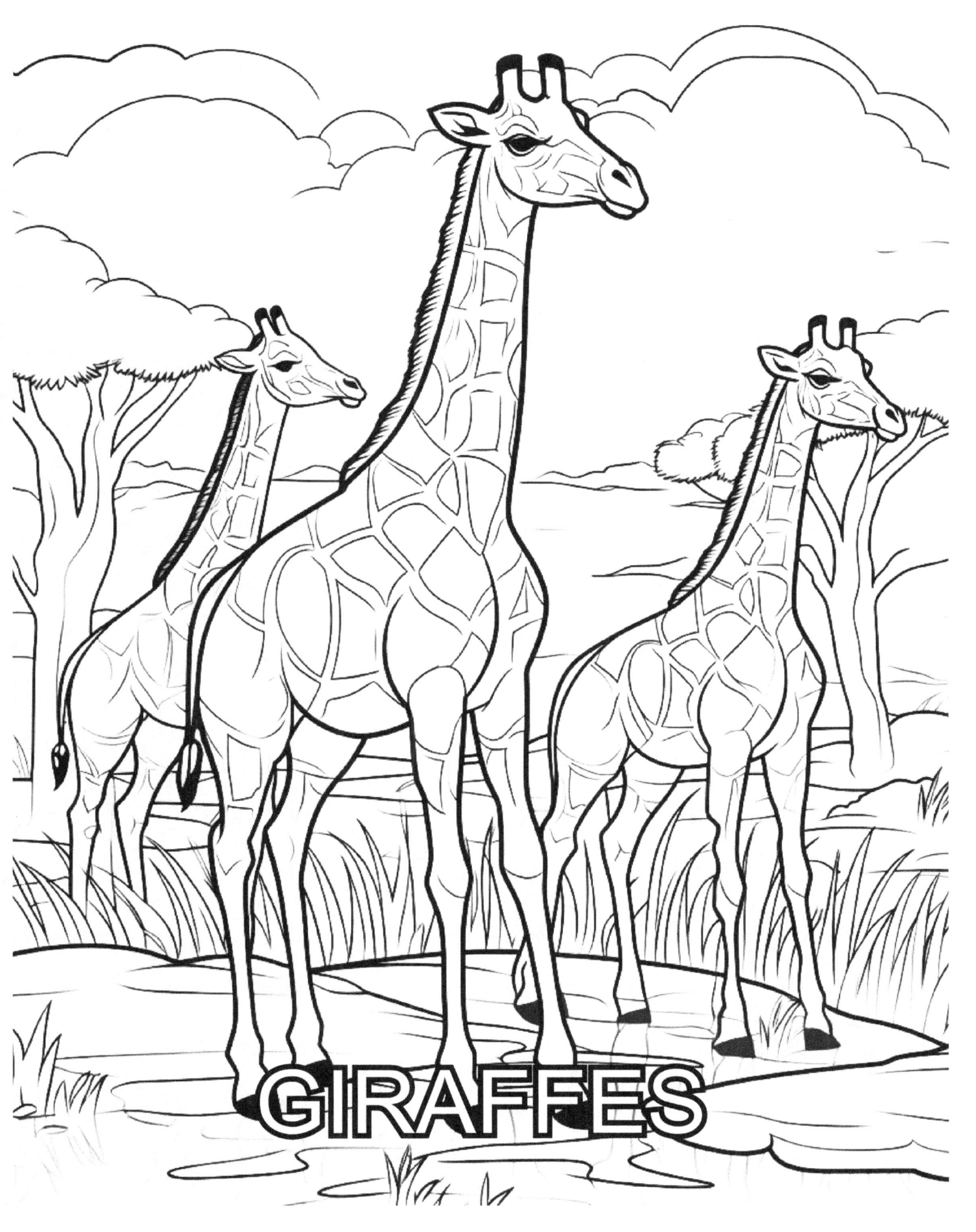

GIRAFFES

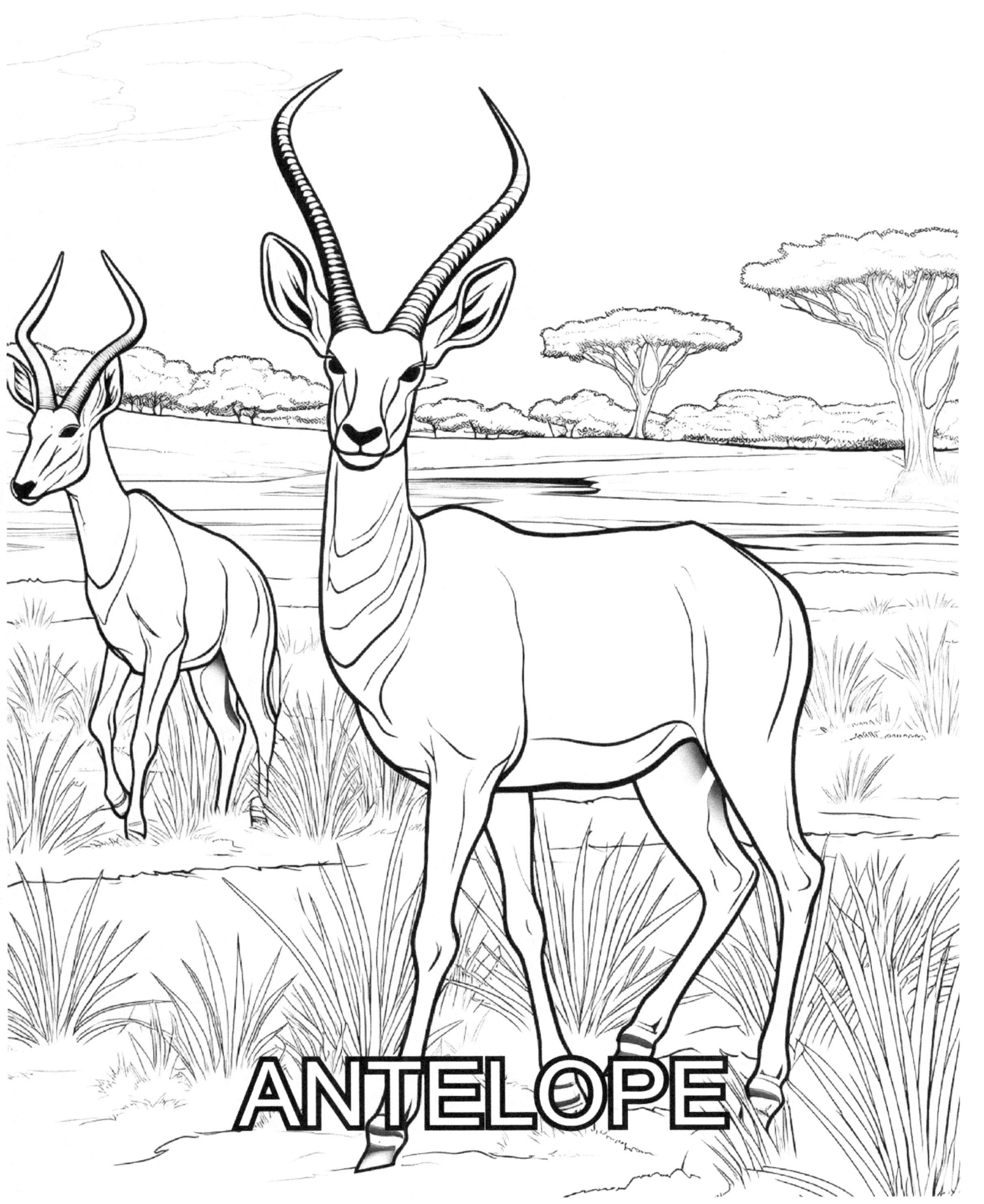

Reviews help spread the word so we can make a bigger impact.
Please take a moment and tell us what you like about the coloring
book by scanning the QR code!

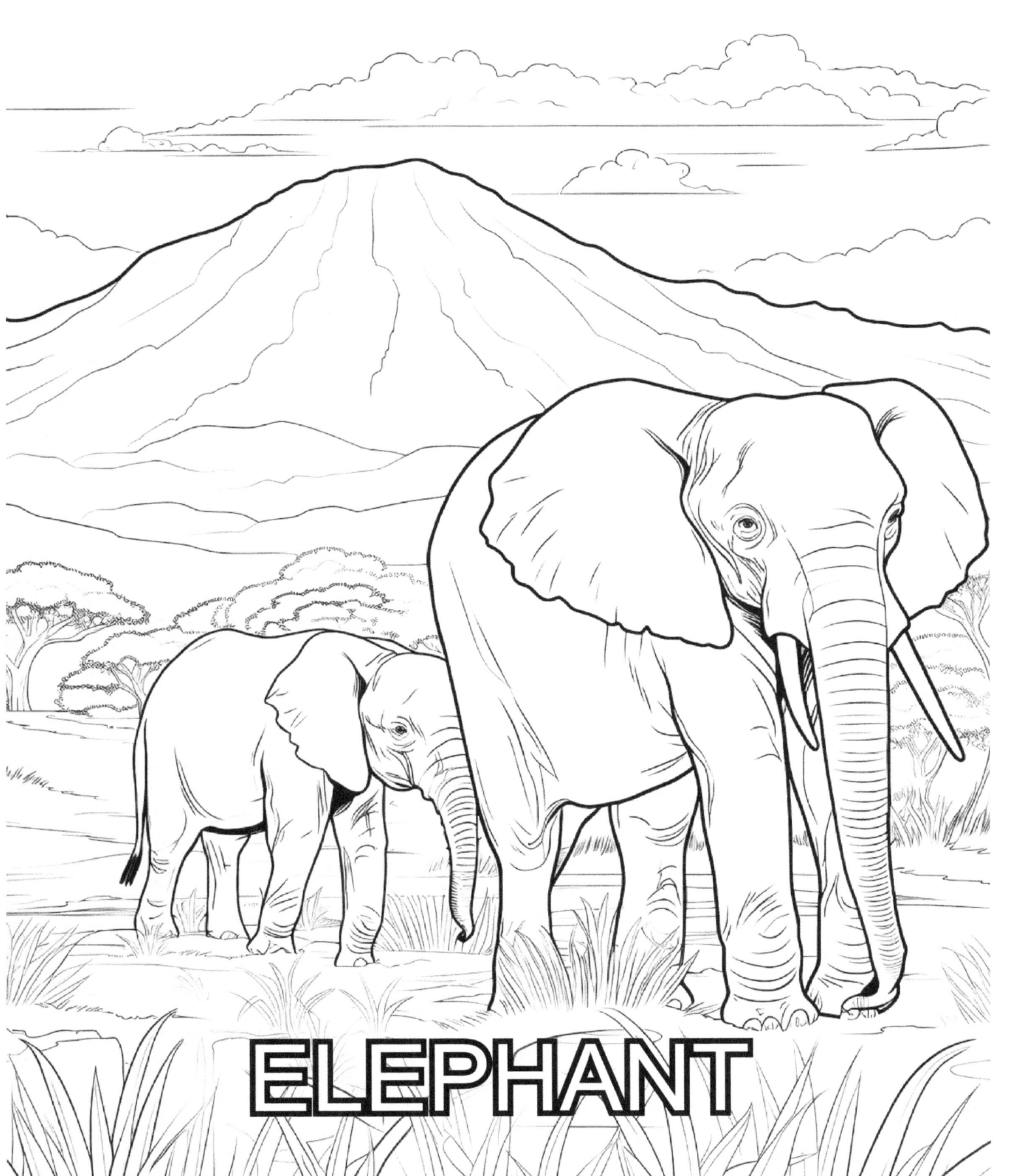

ELEPHANT

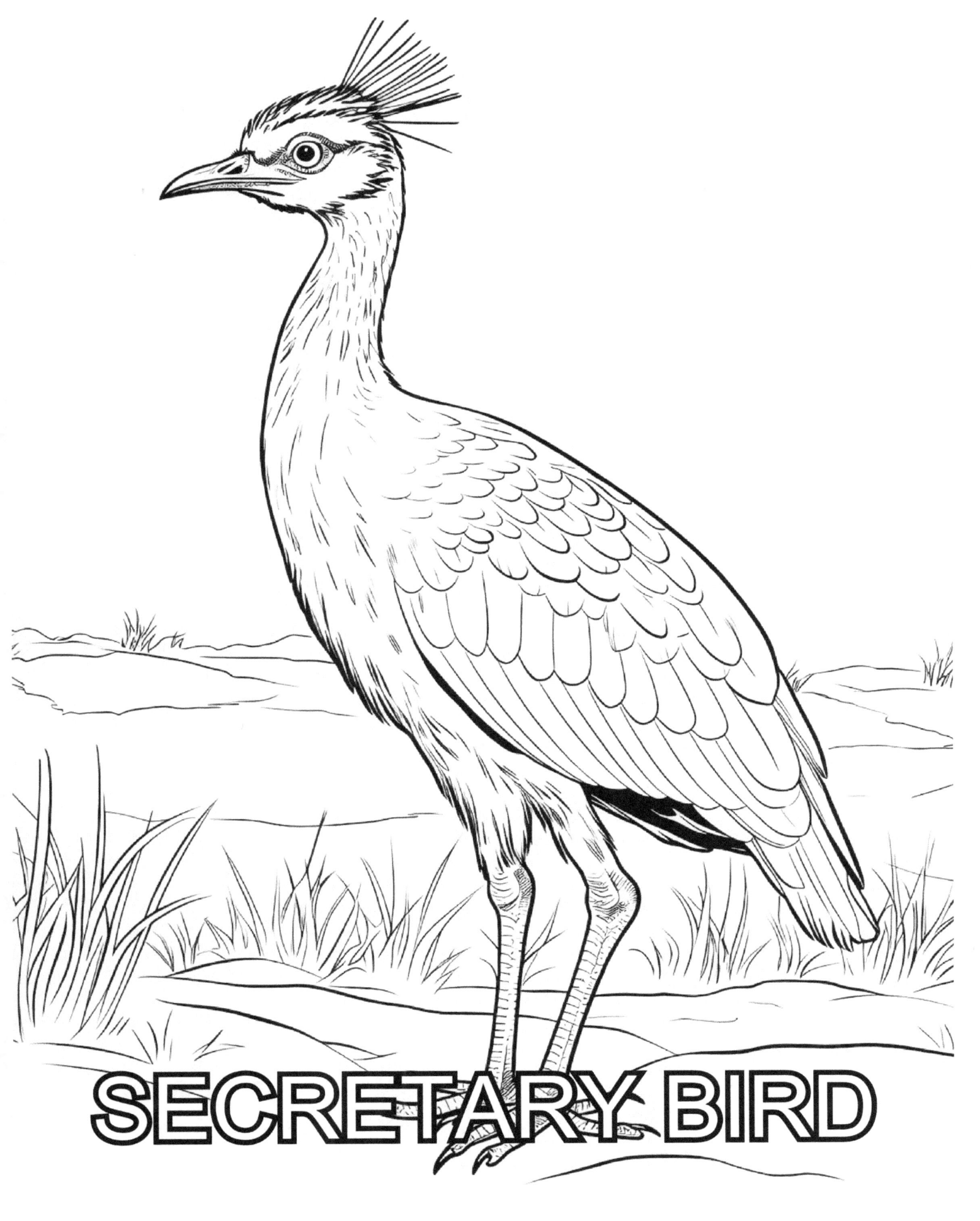

SECRETARY BIRD

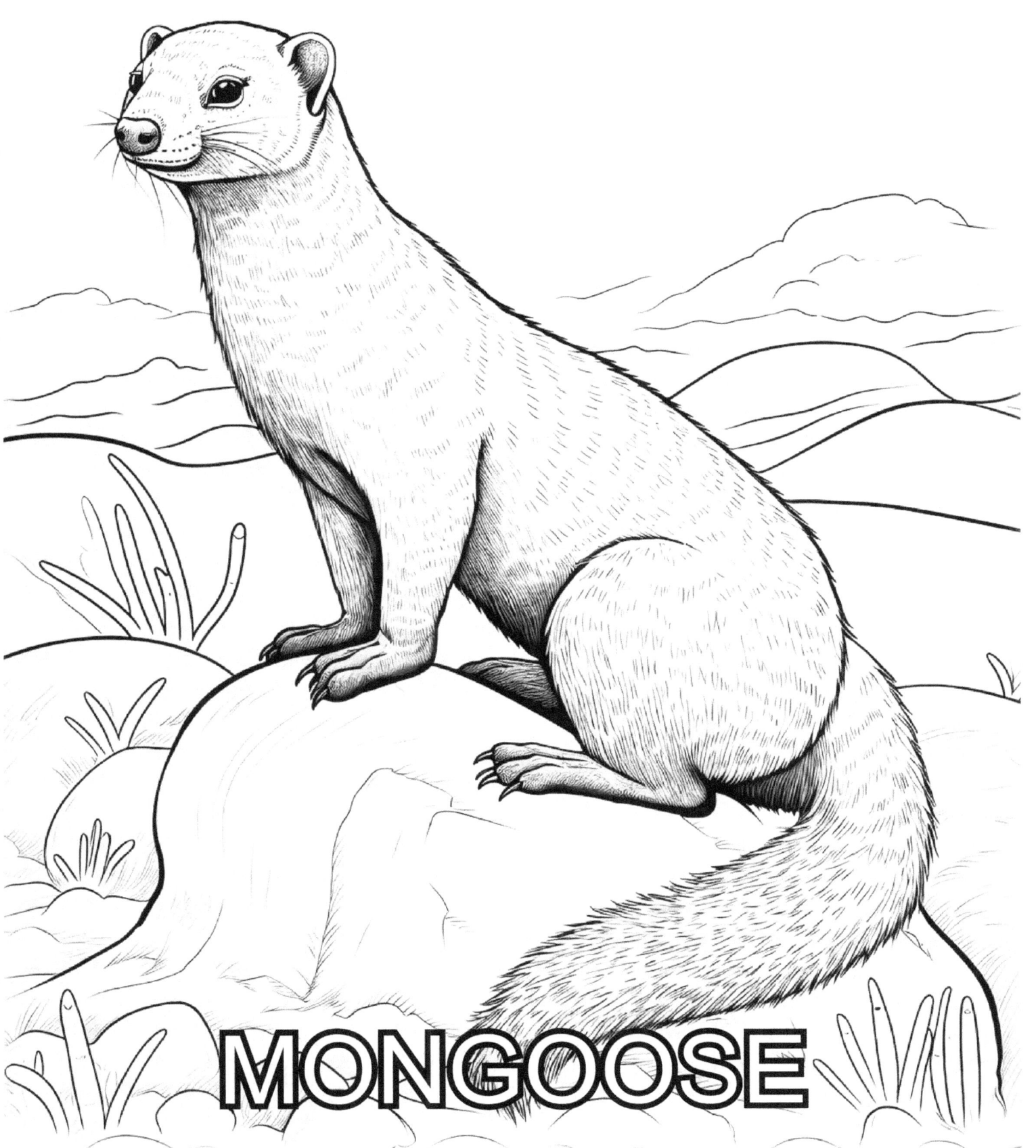

MONGOOSE

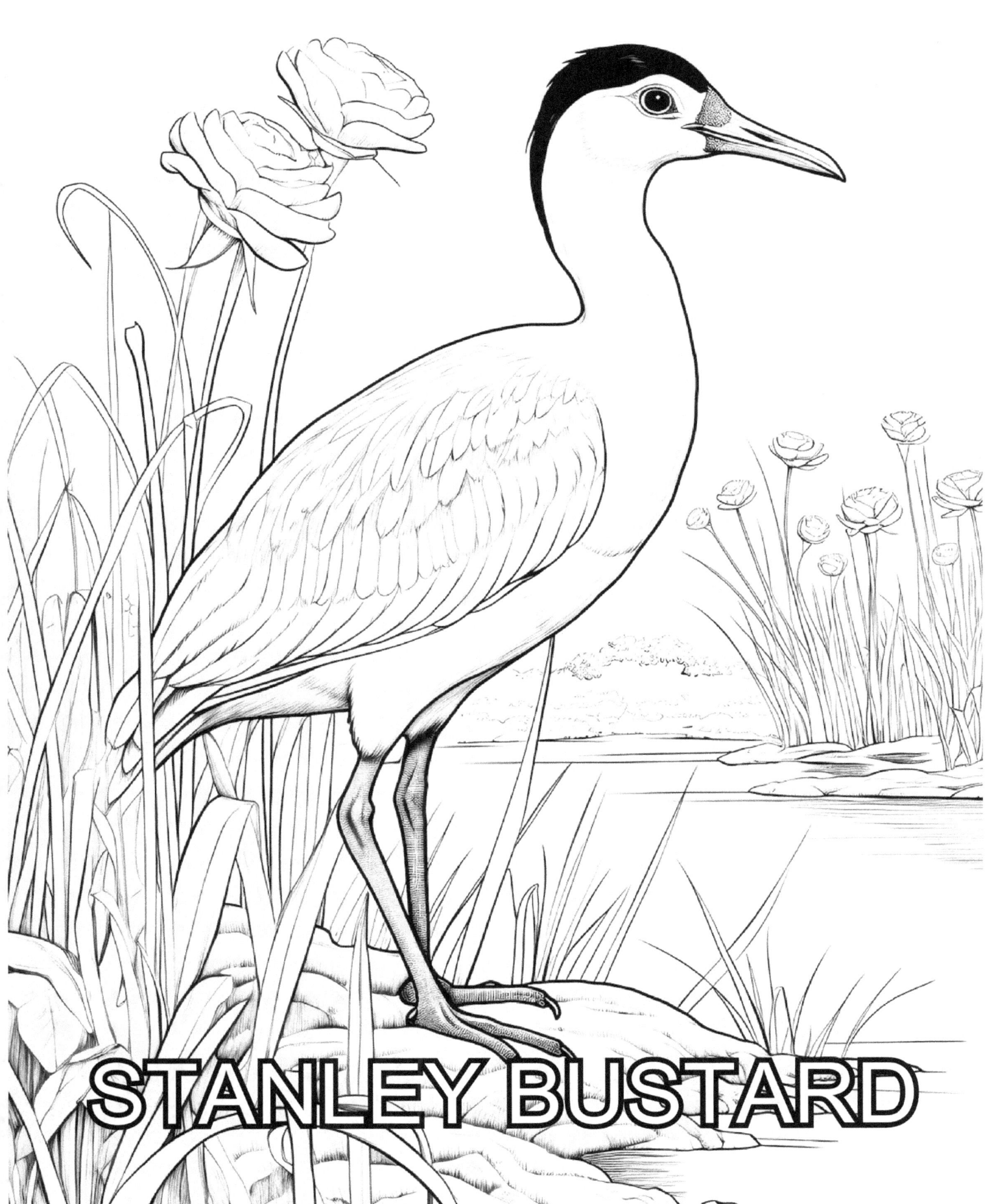

STANLEY BUSTARD

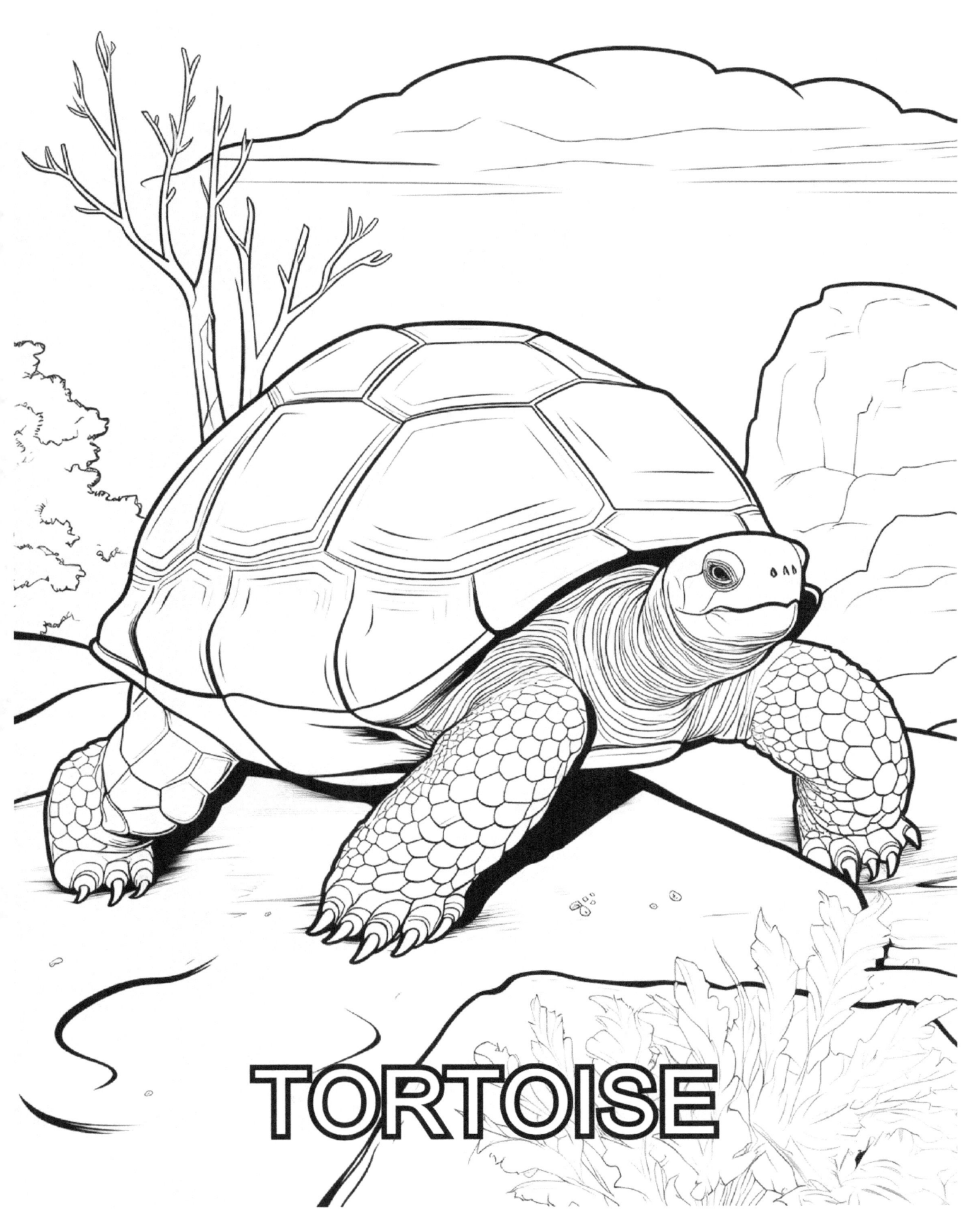

TORTOISE

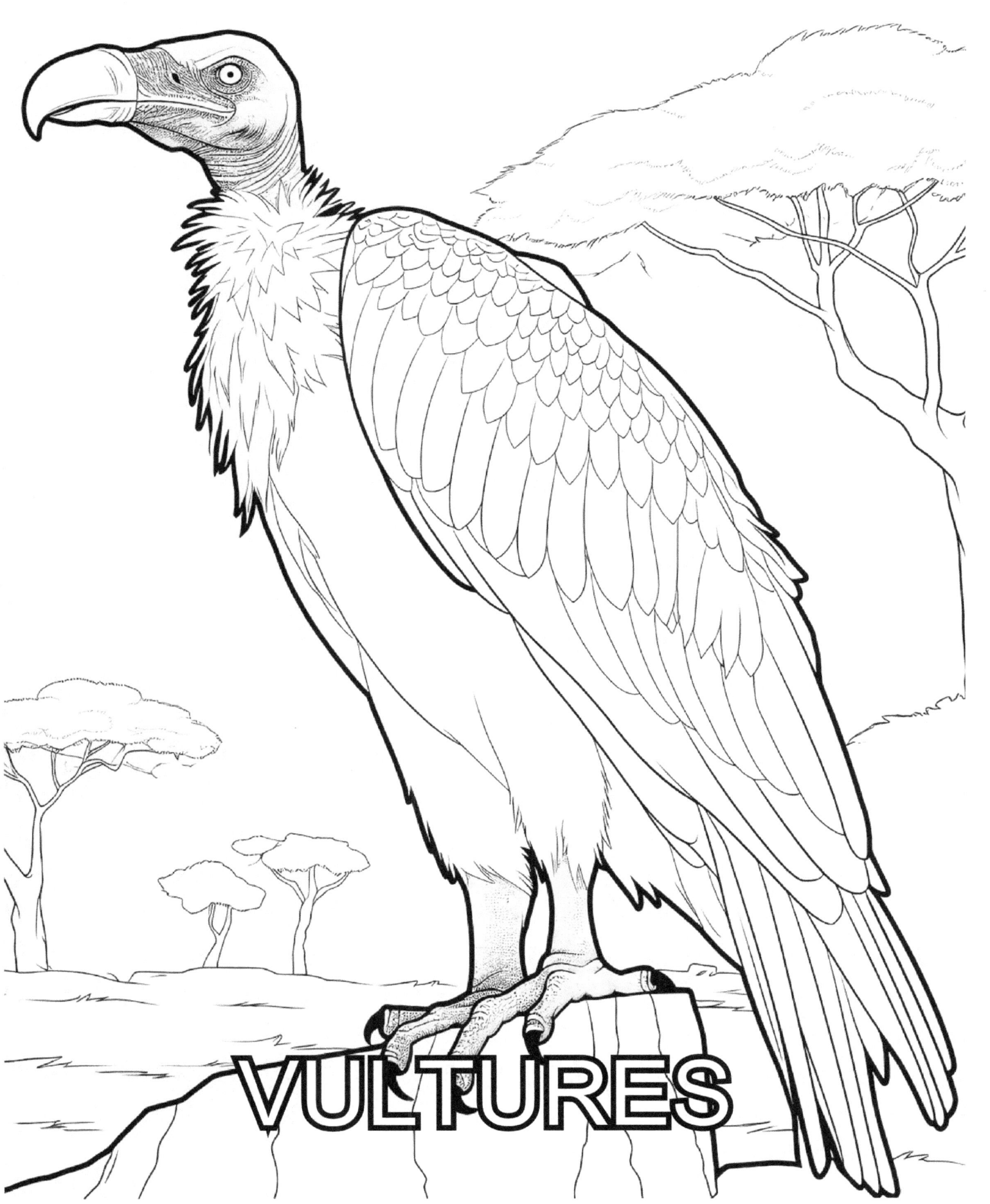

VULTURES

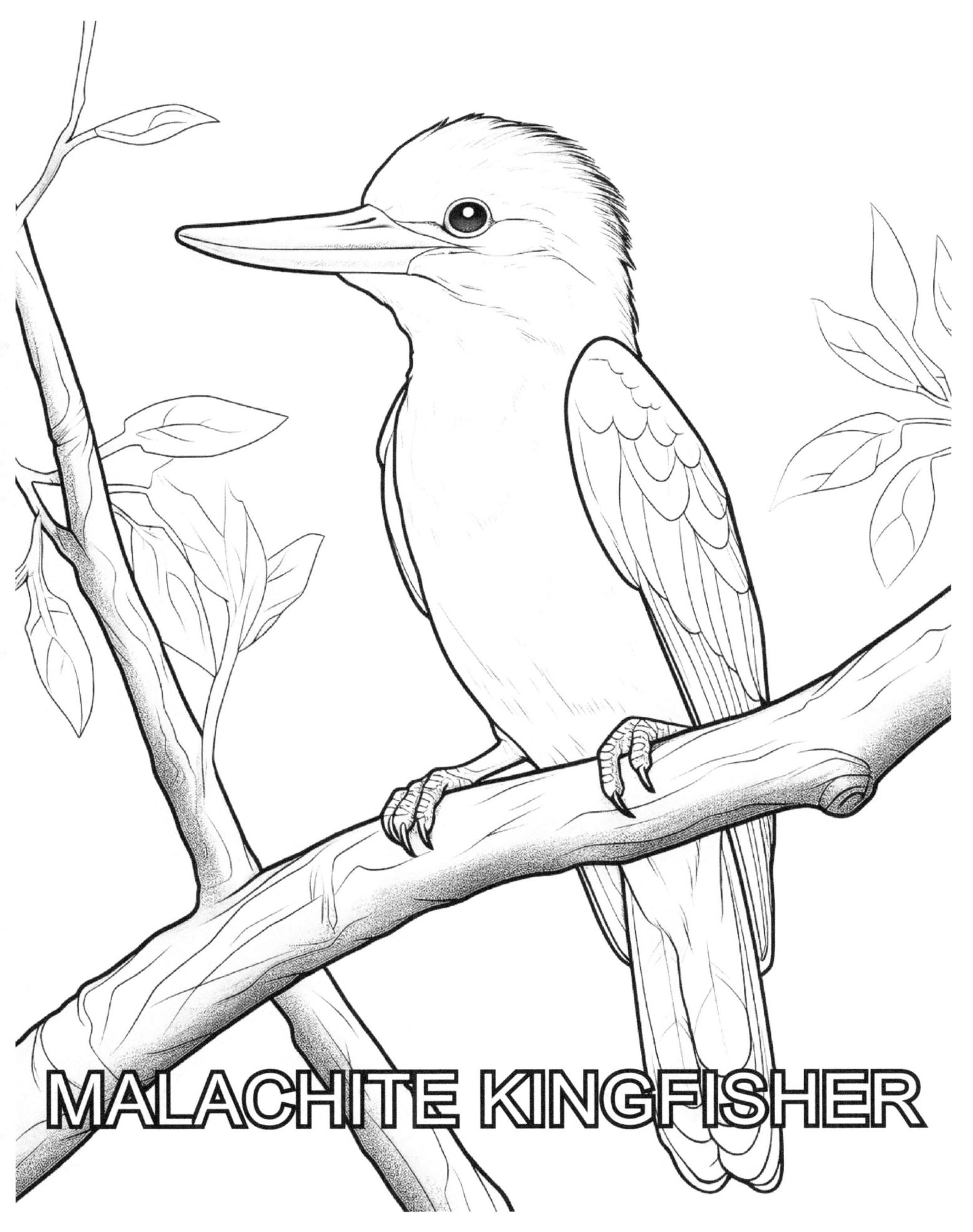

MALACHITE KINGFISHER

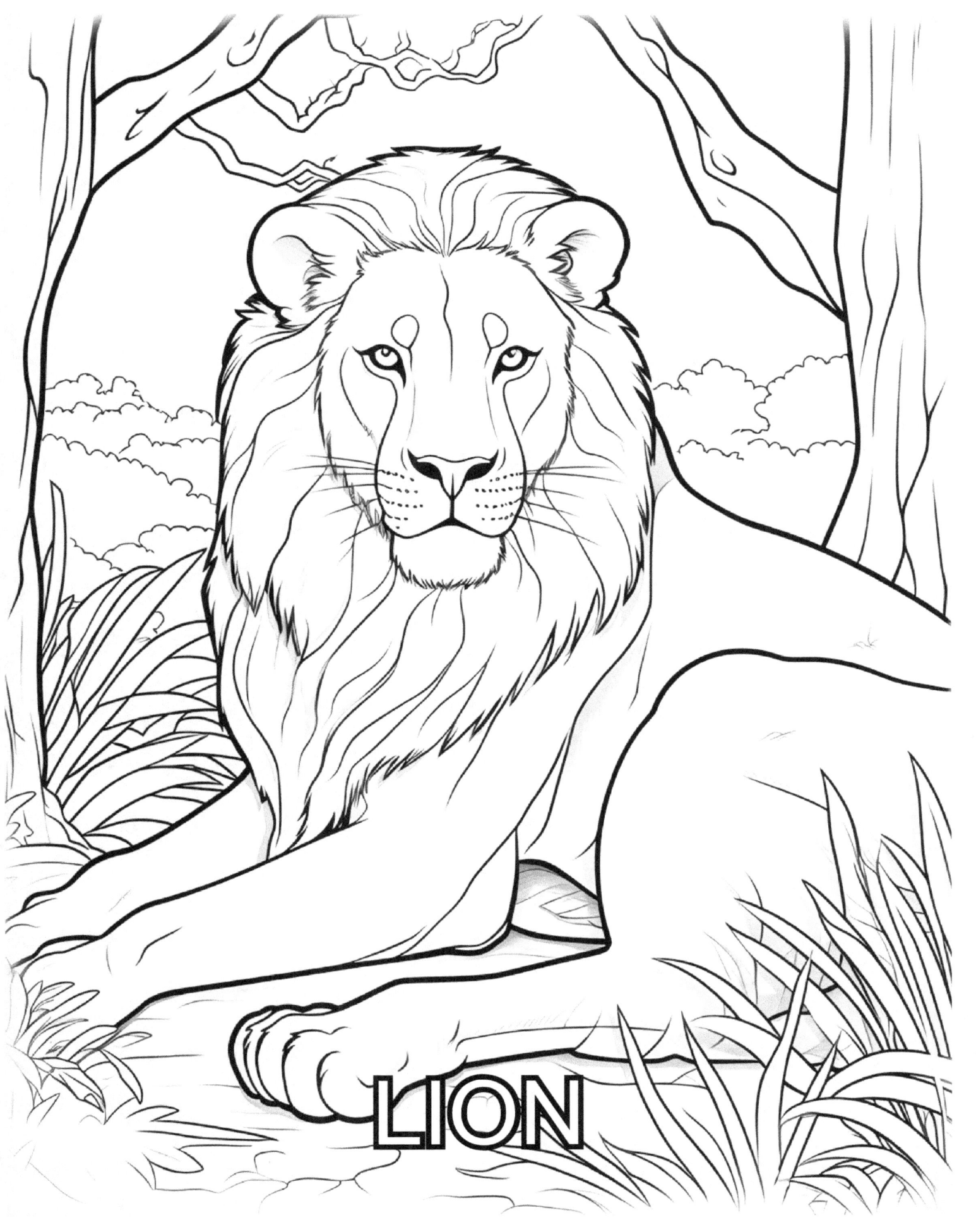

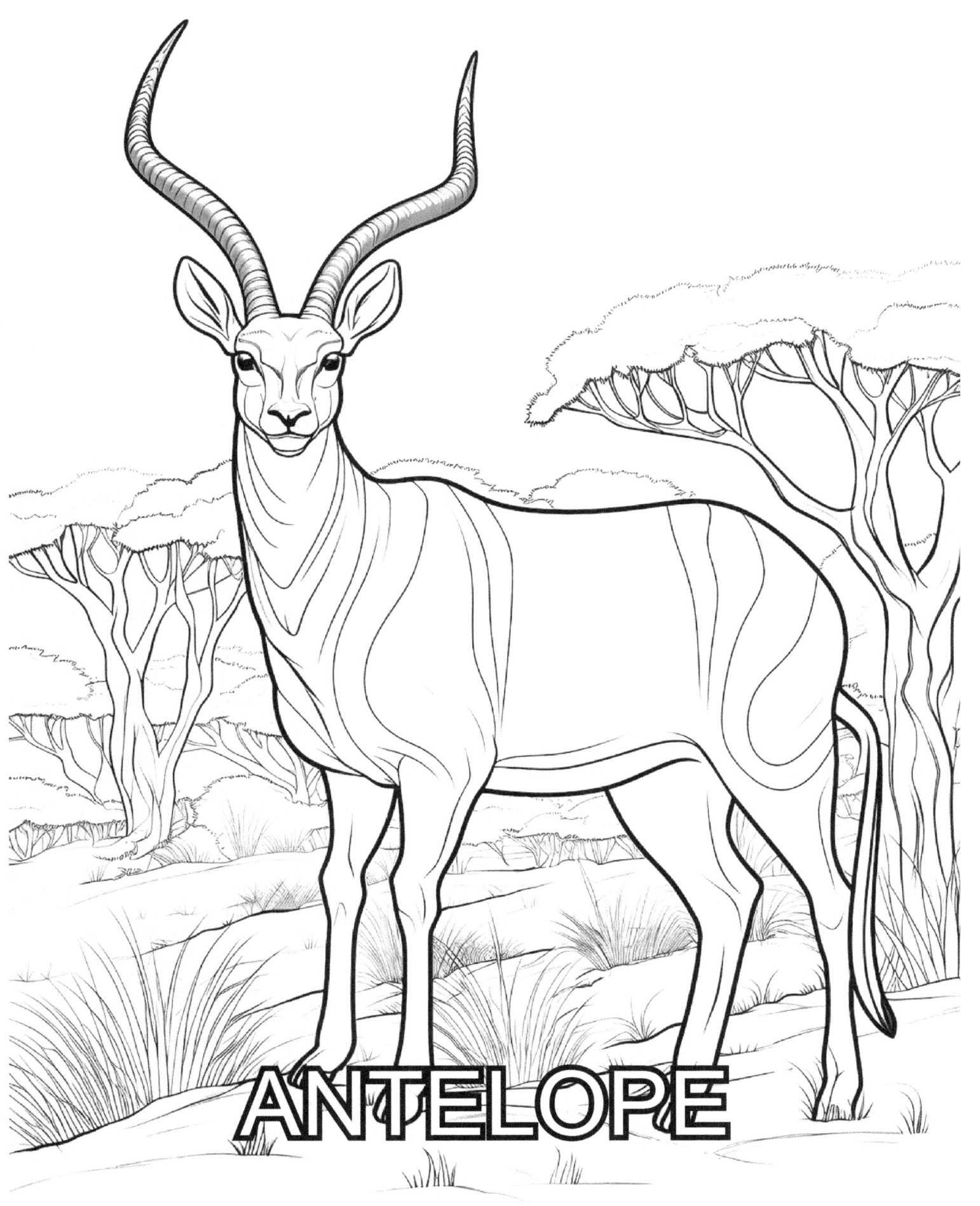

ANTELOPE

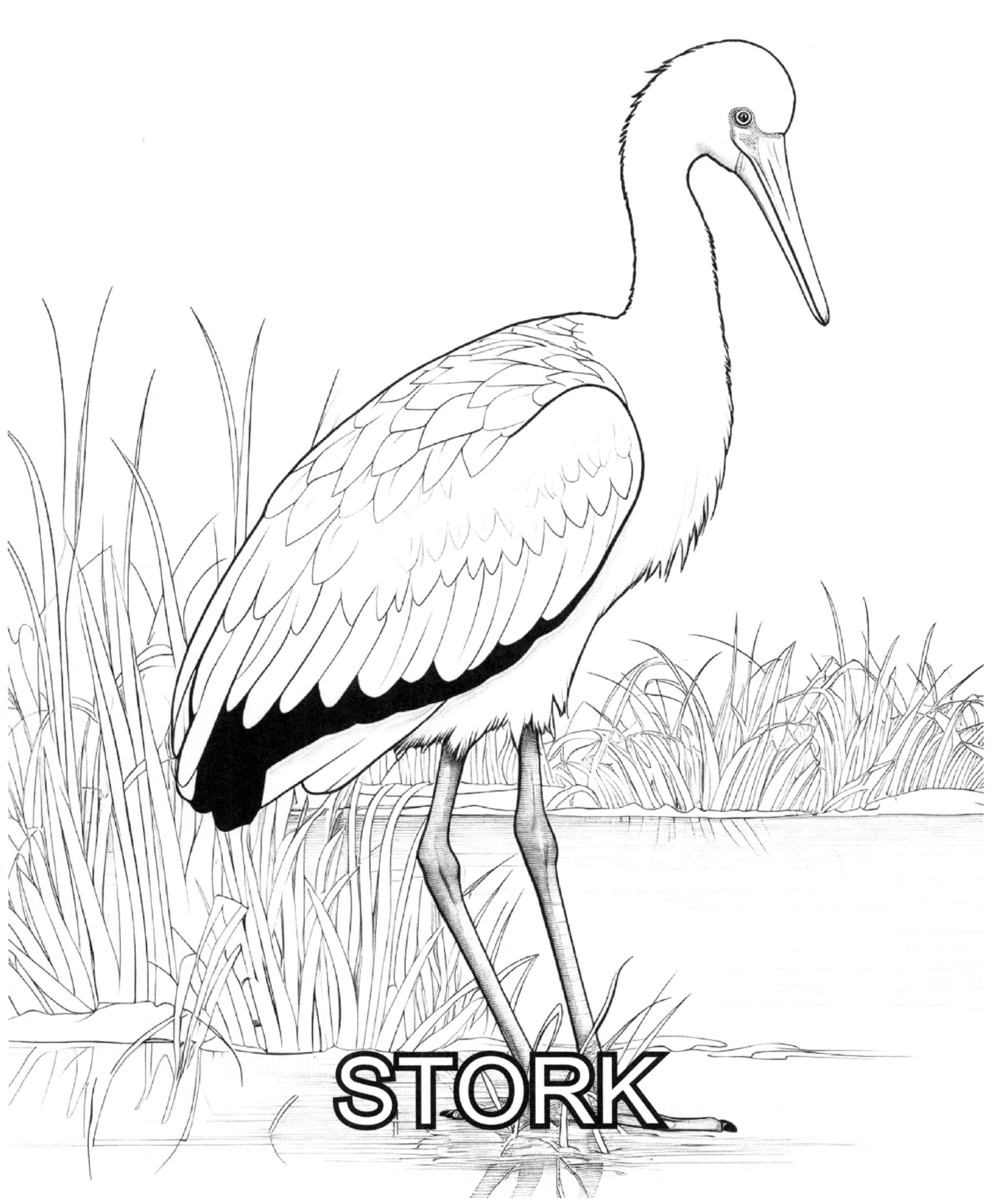

STORK

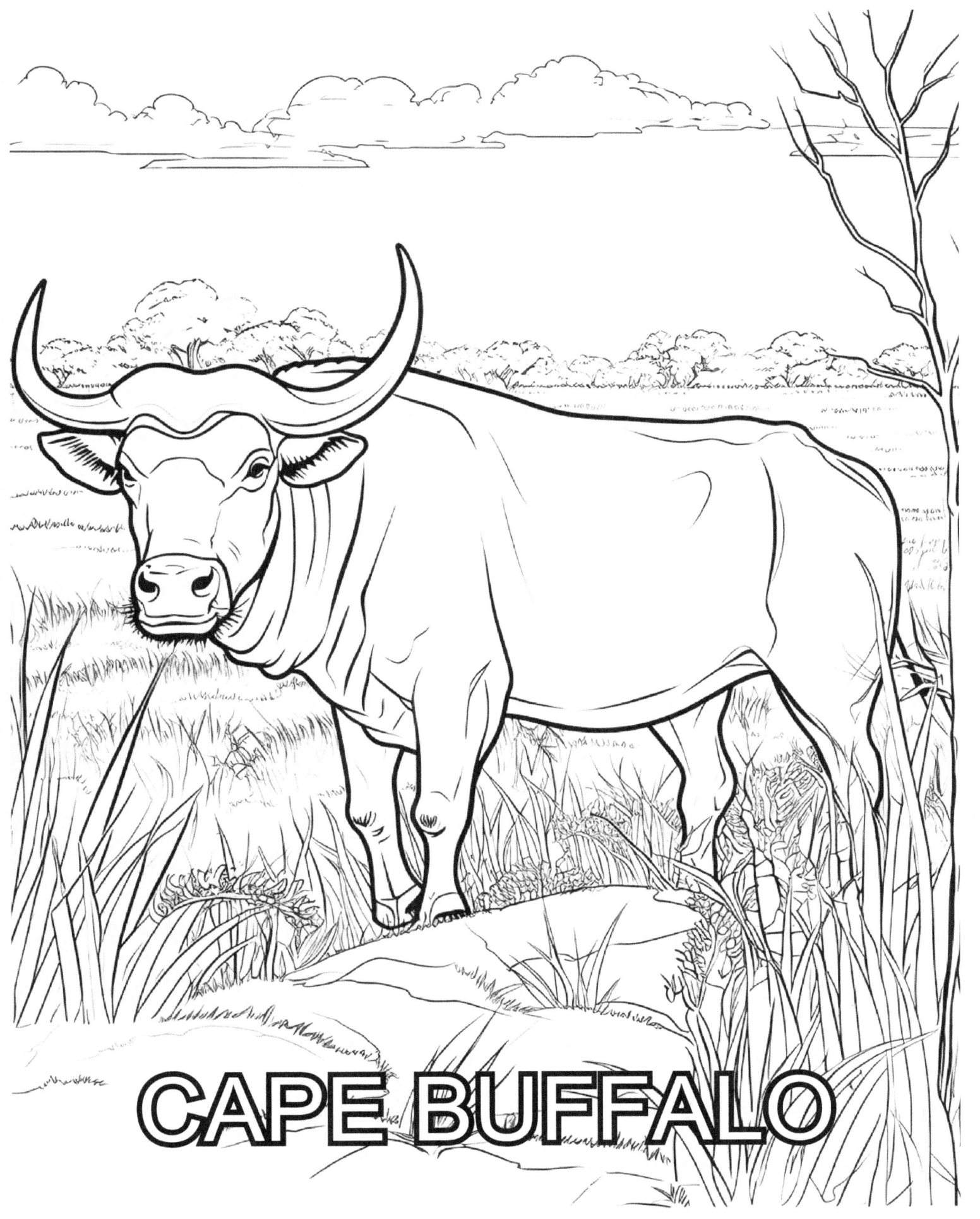

CAPE BUFFALO

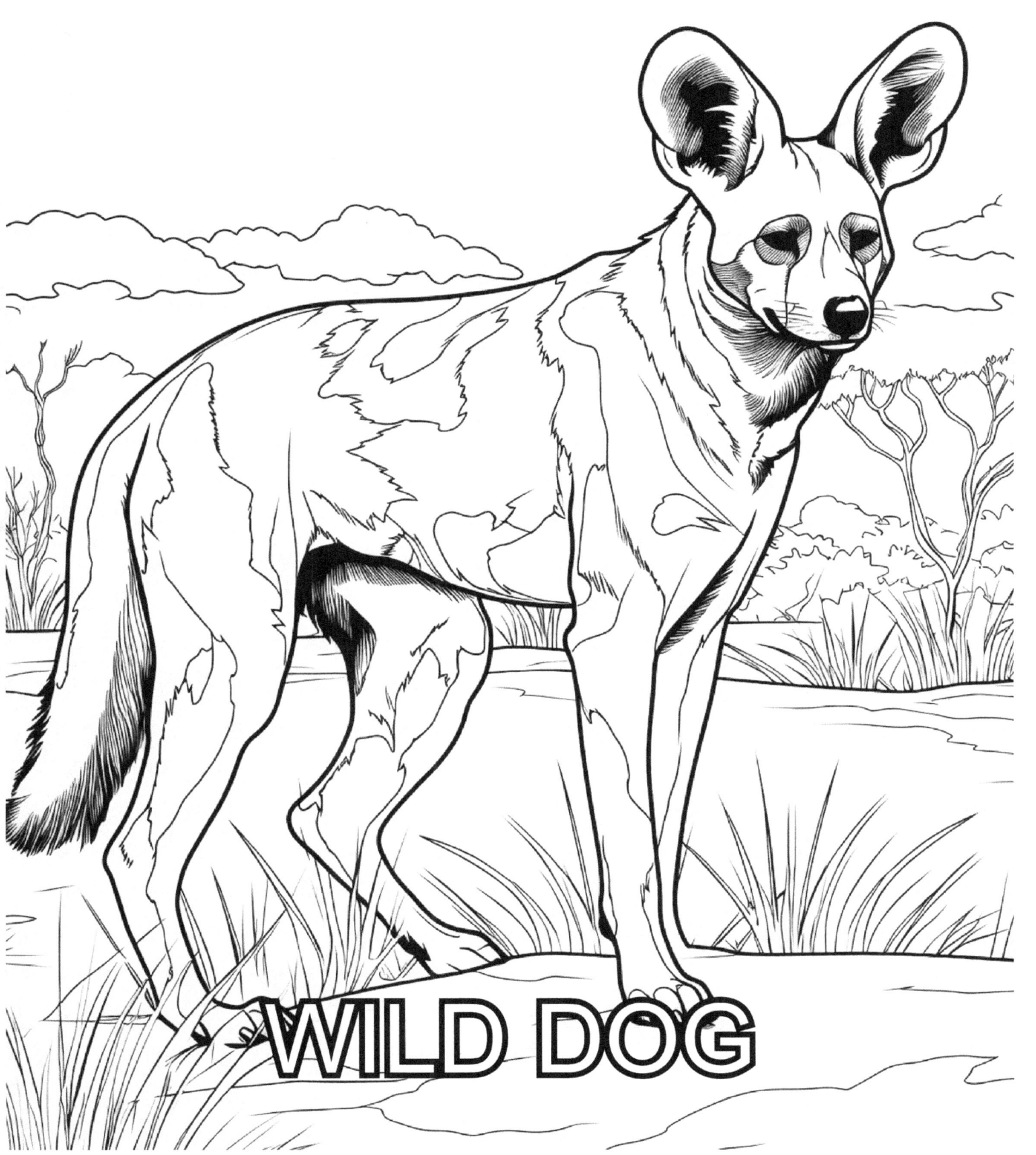

WILD DOG

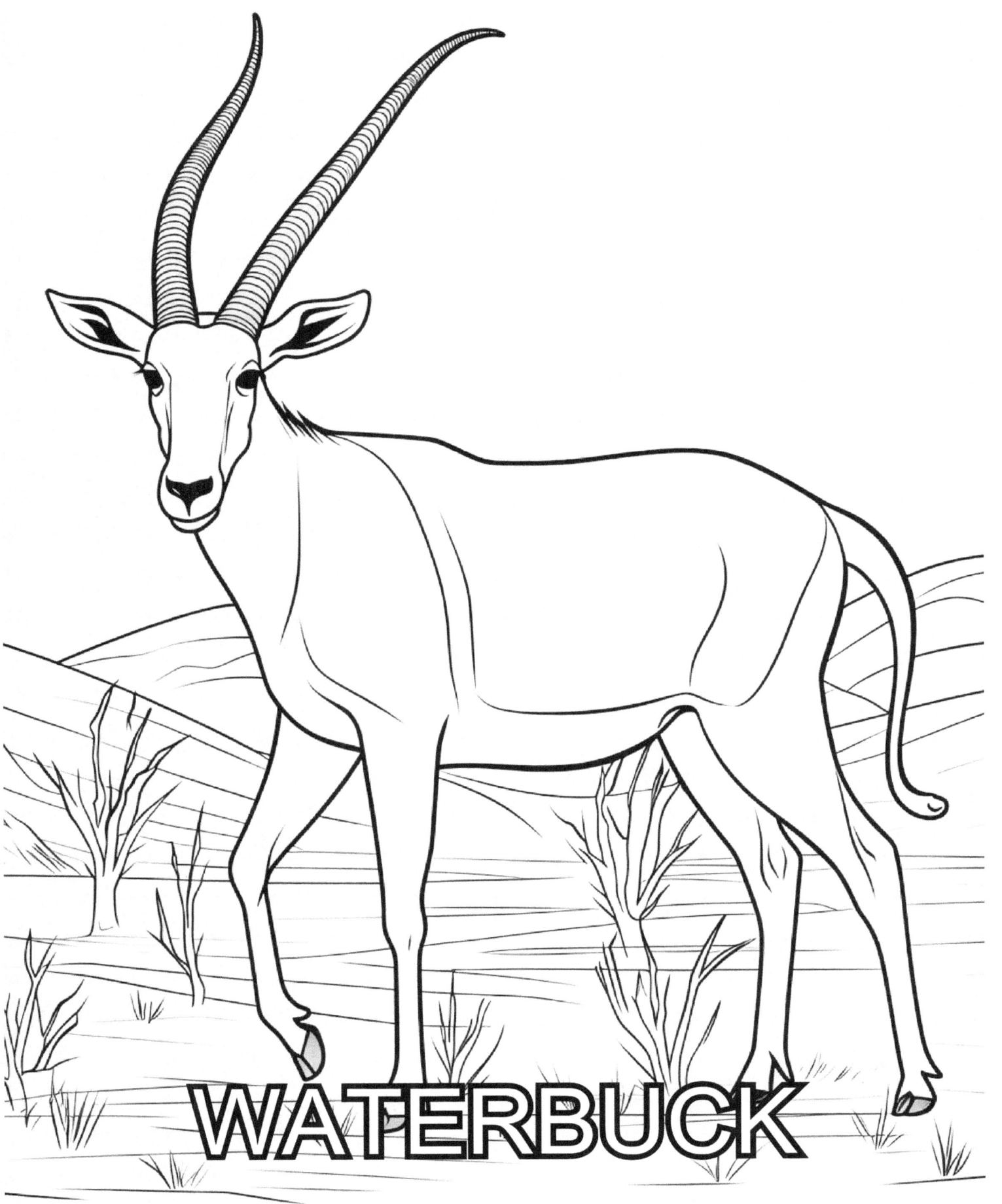

WATERBUCK

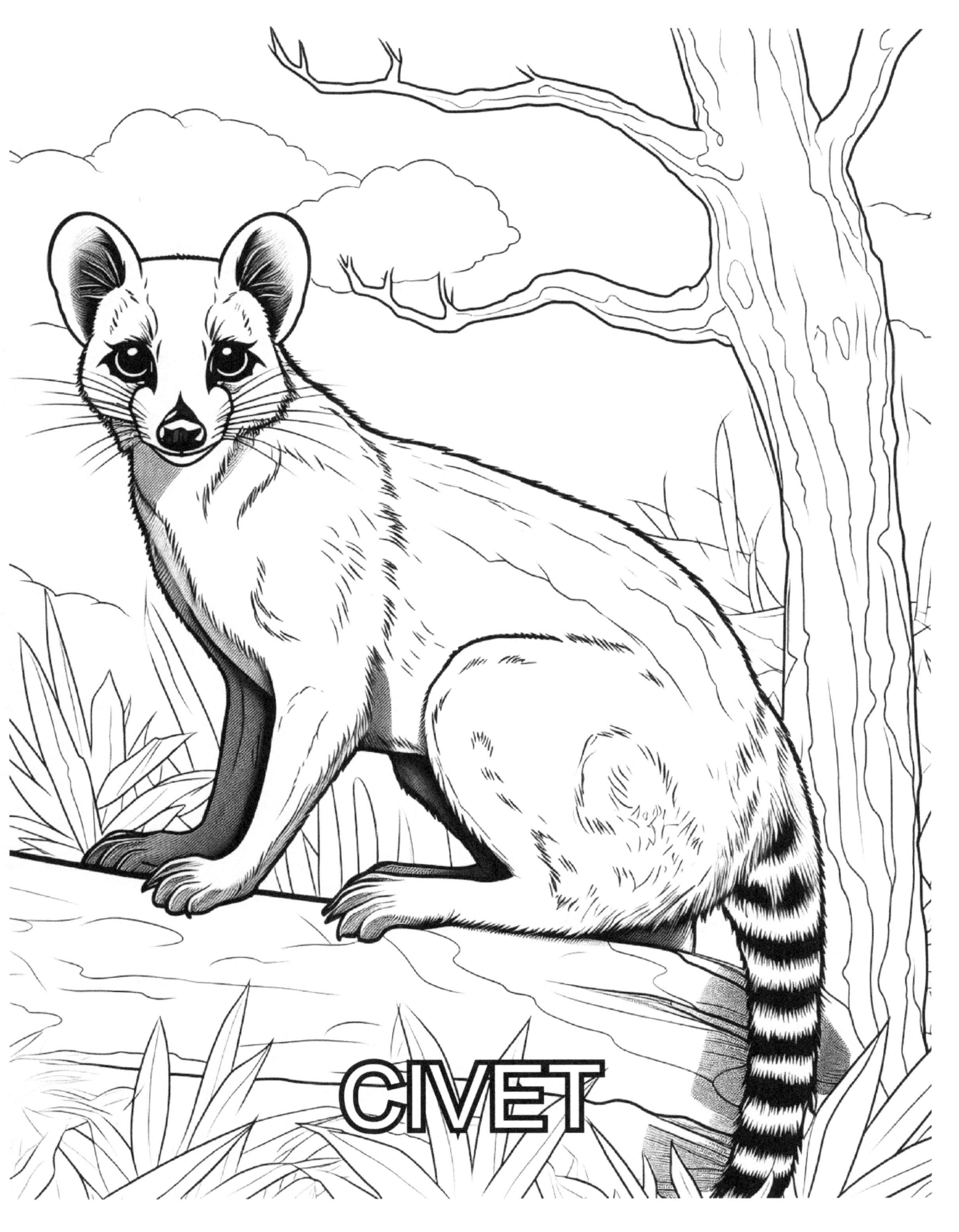

CIVET

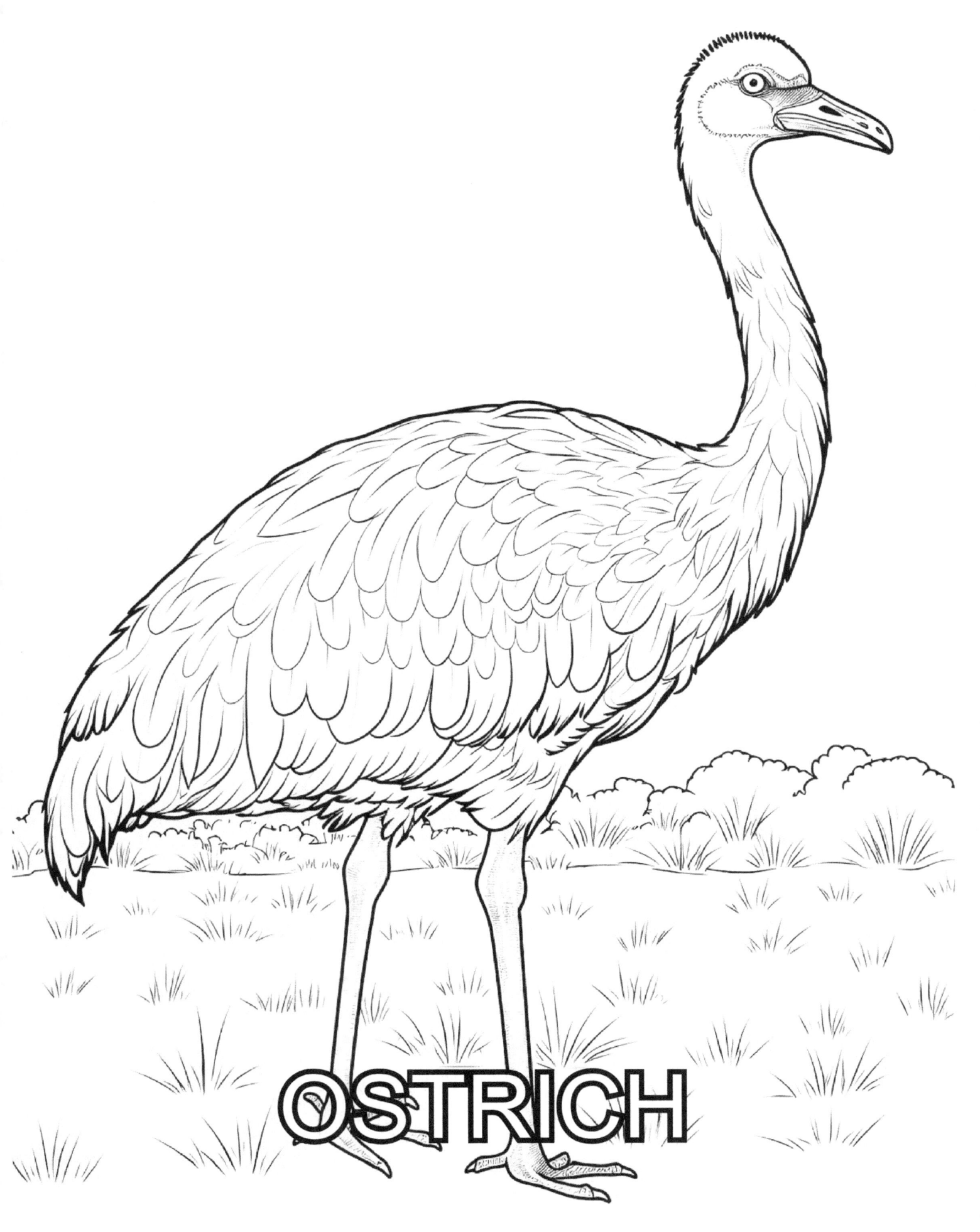

OSTRICH

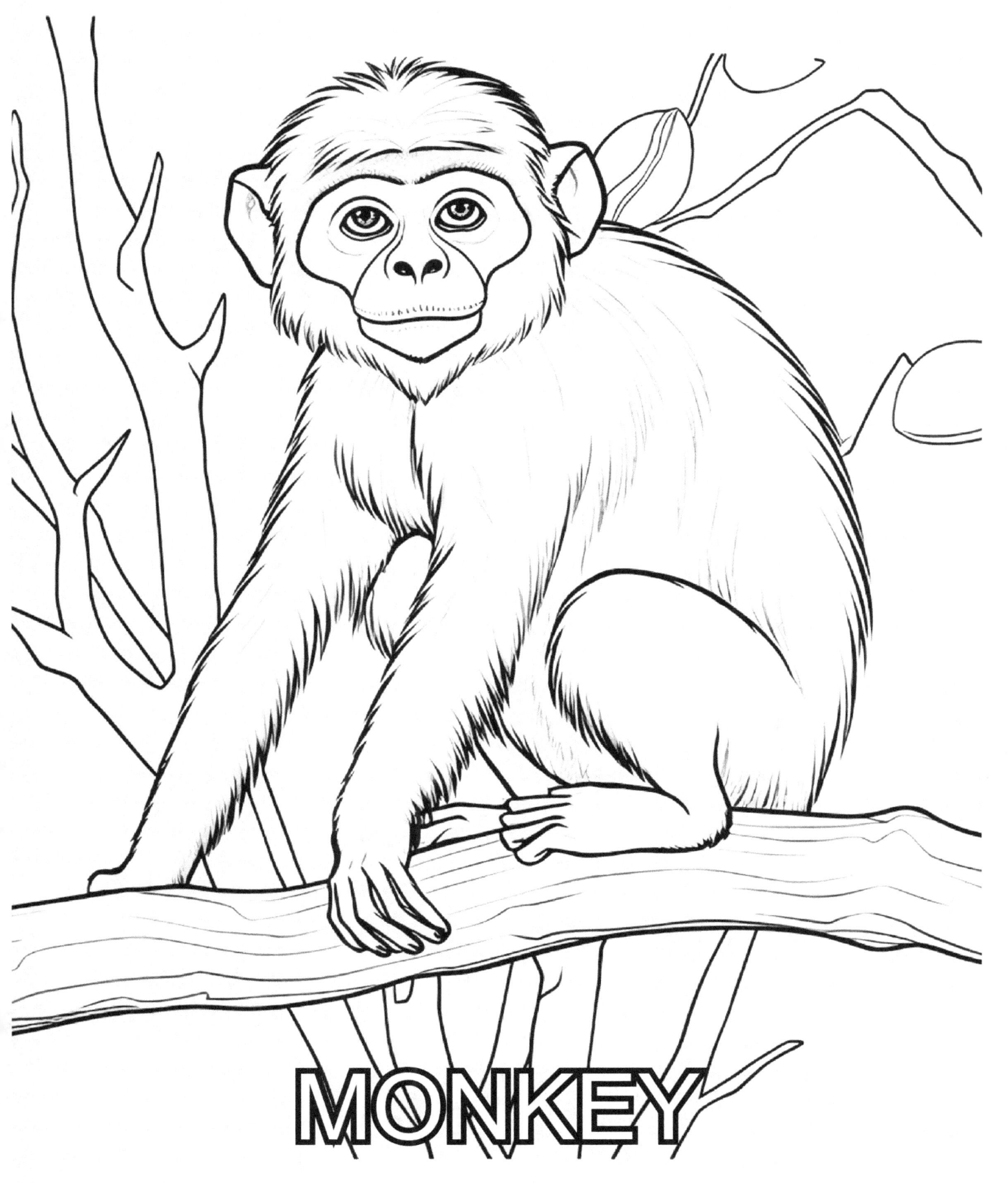

MONKEY

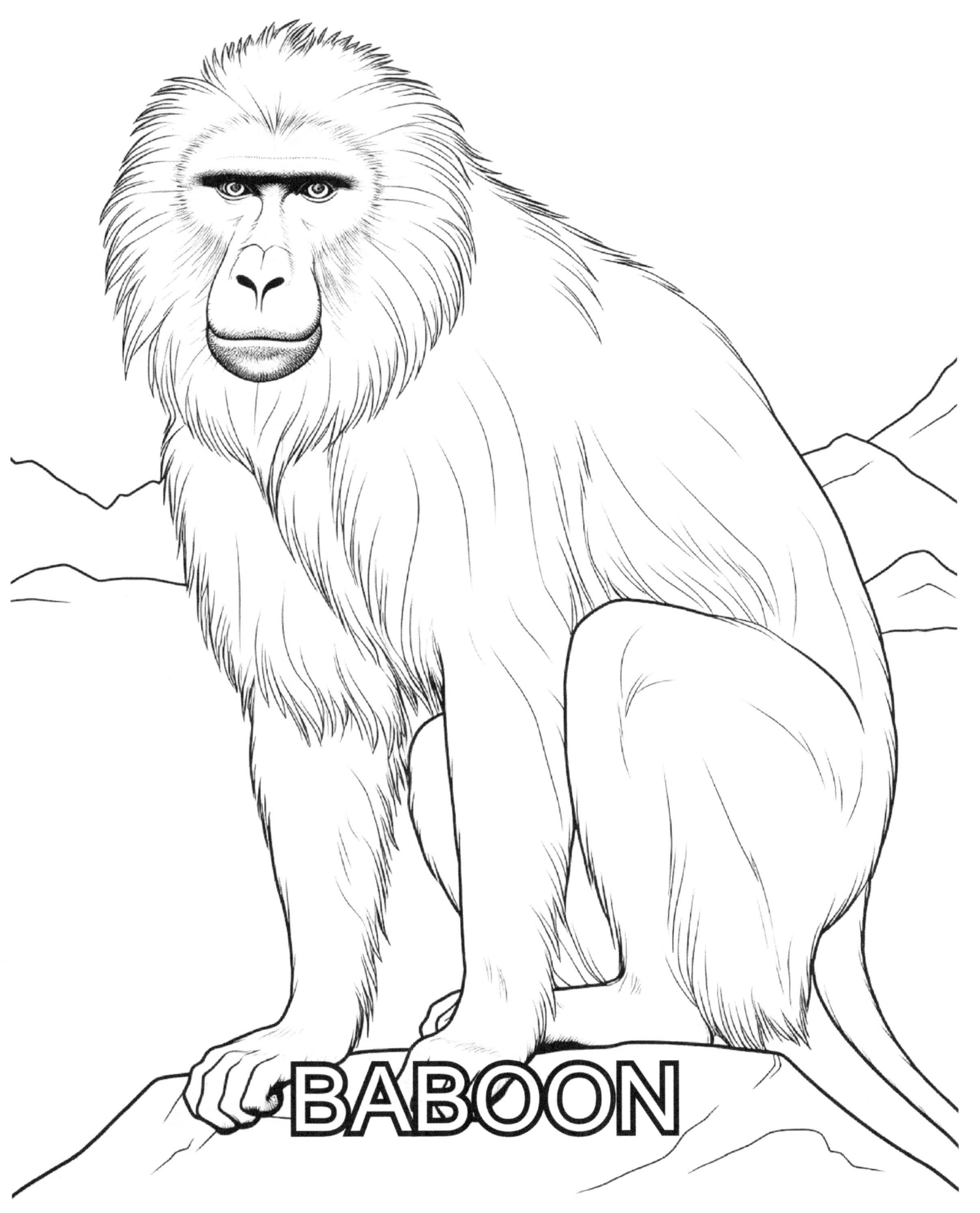

BABOON

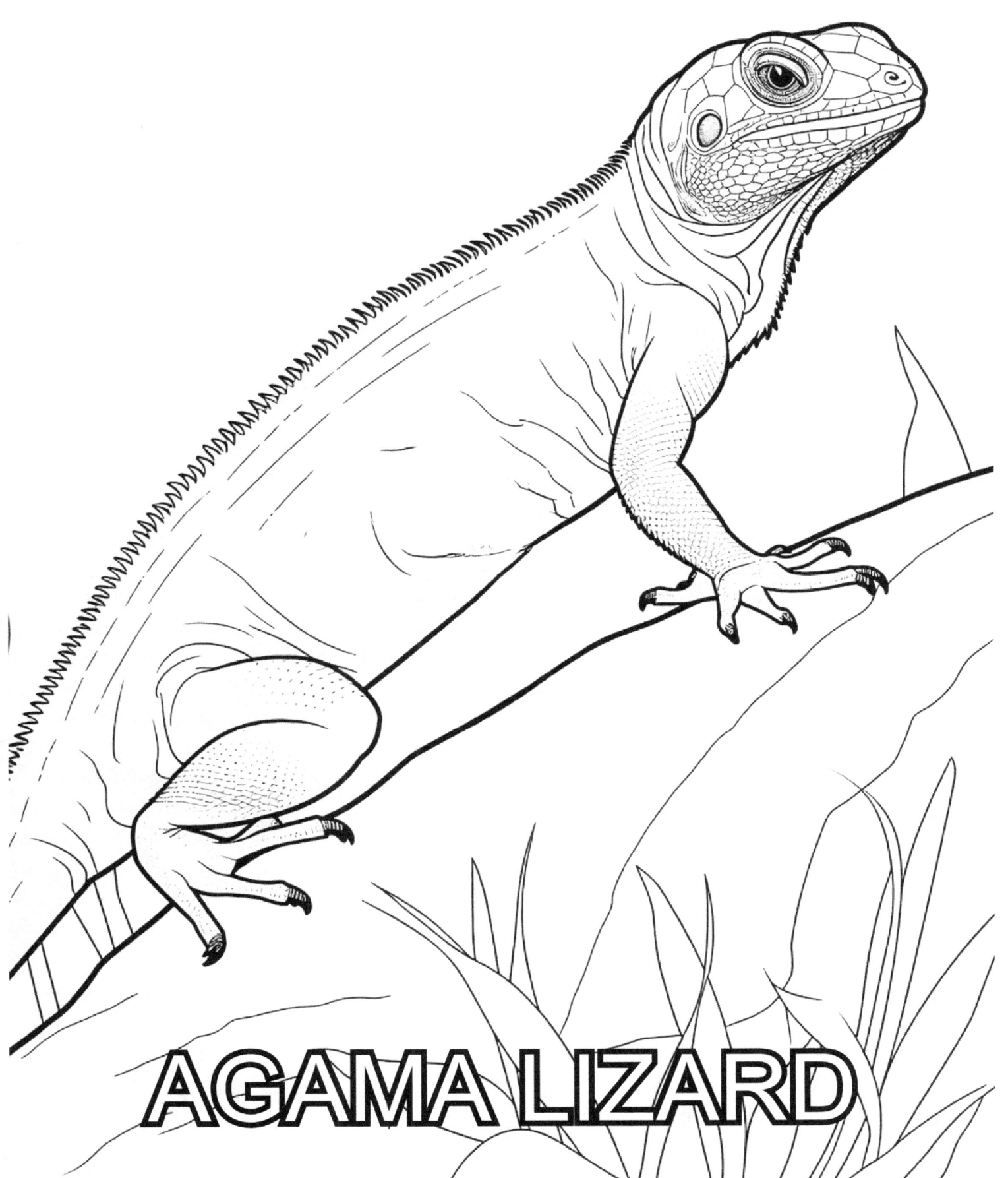

AGAMA LIZARD

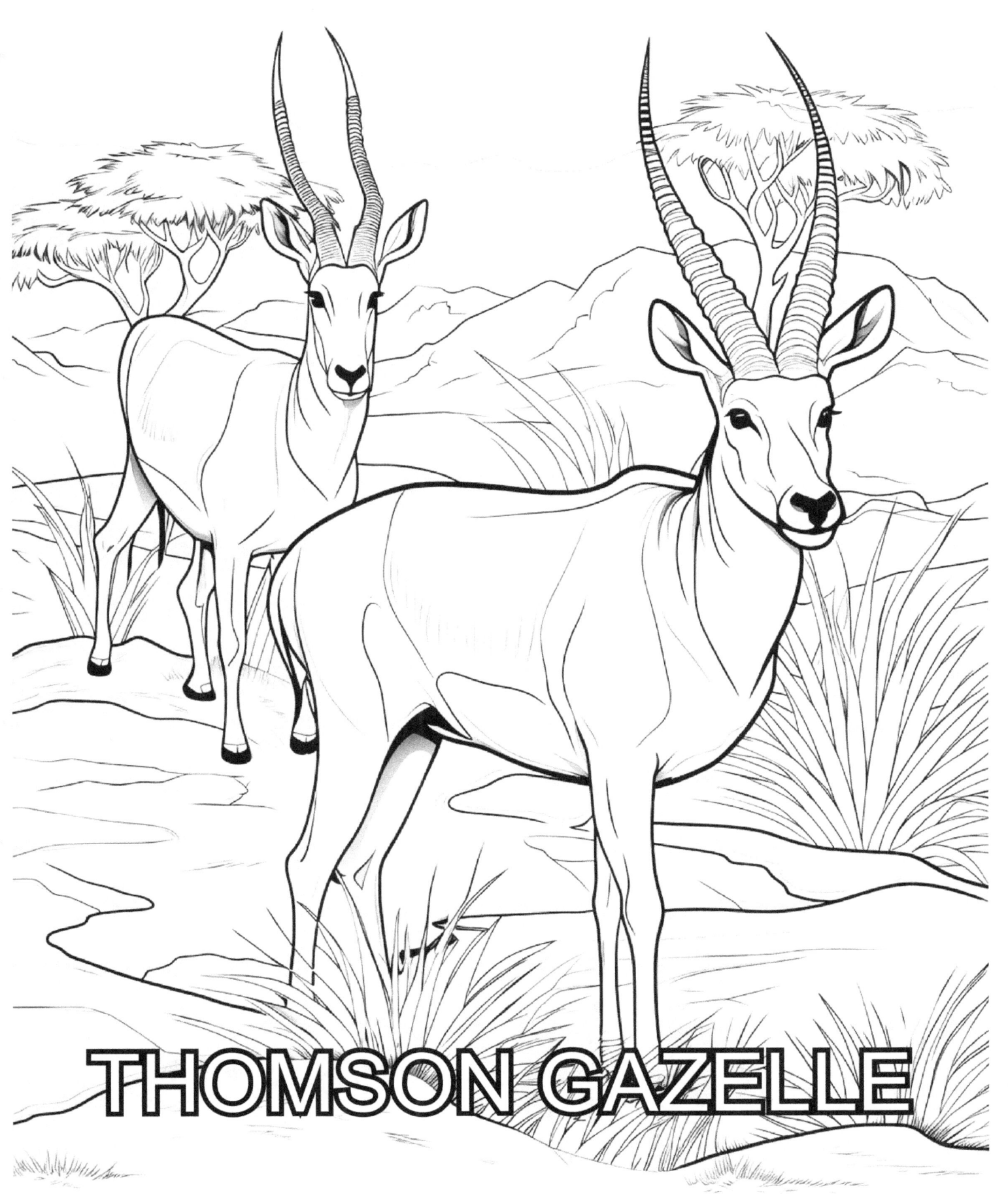

THOMSON GAZELLE

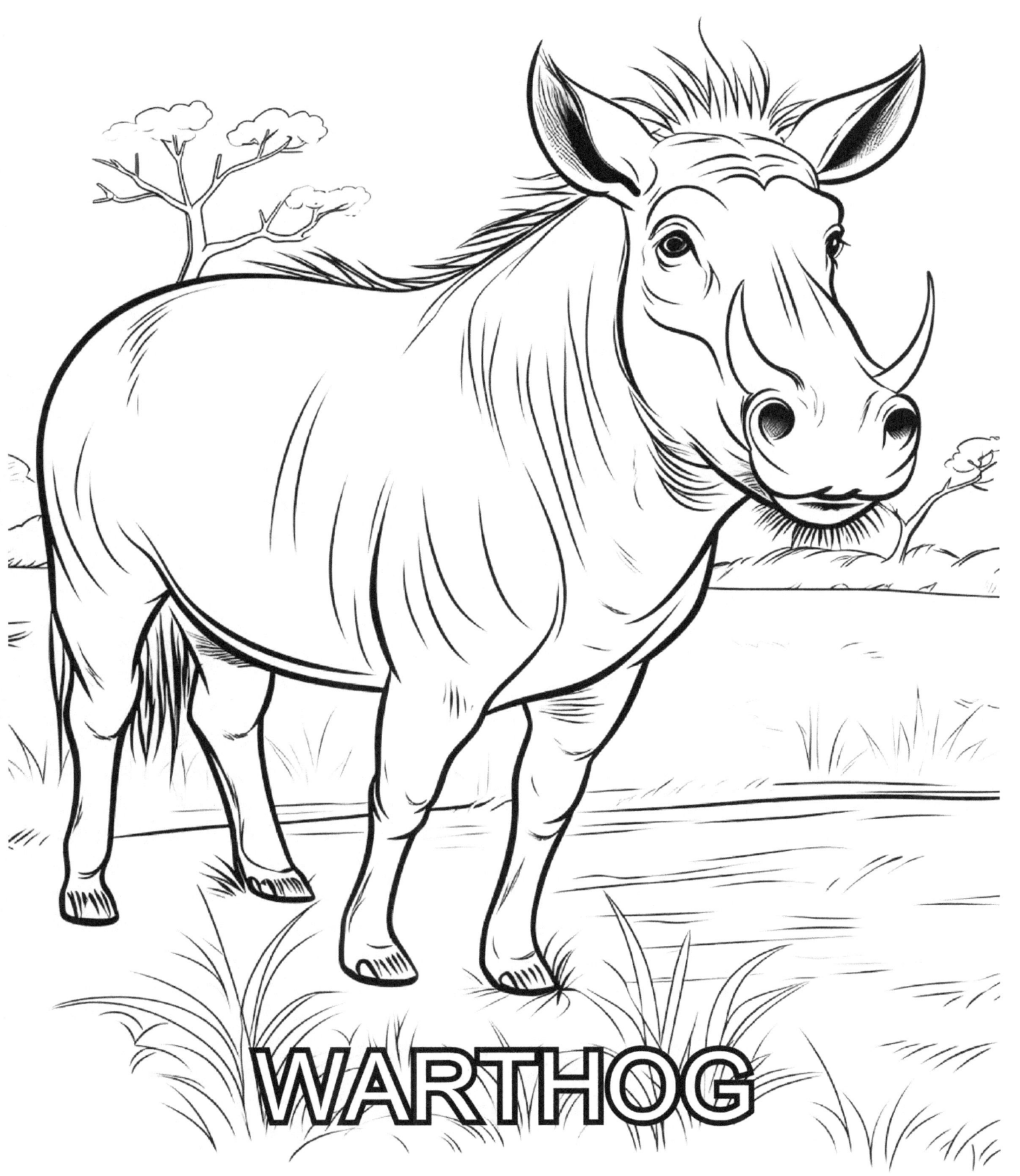

WARTHOG

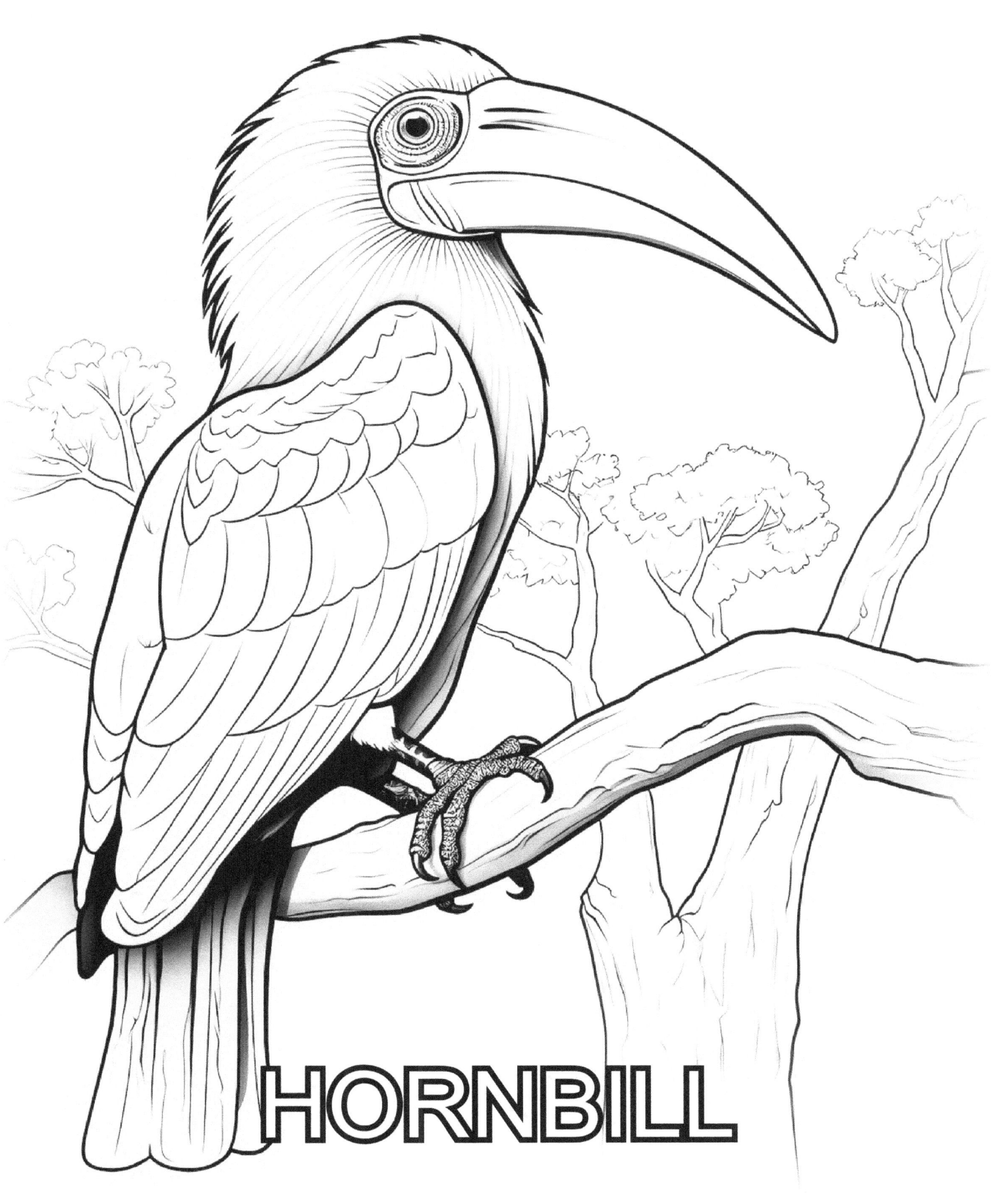

HORNBILL

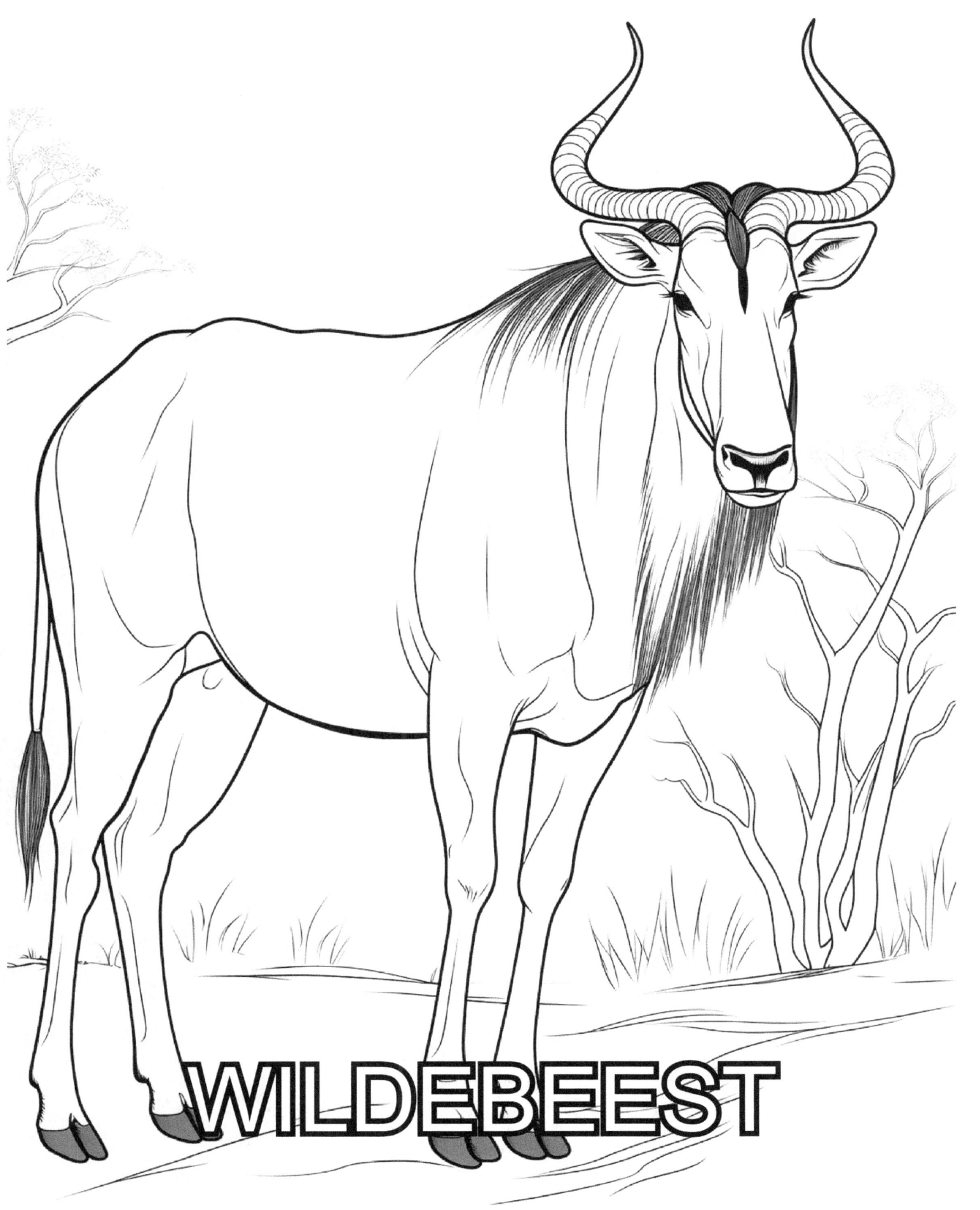

WILDEBEEST

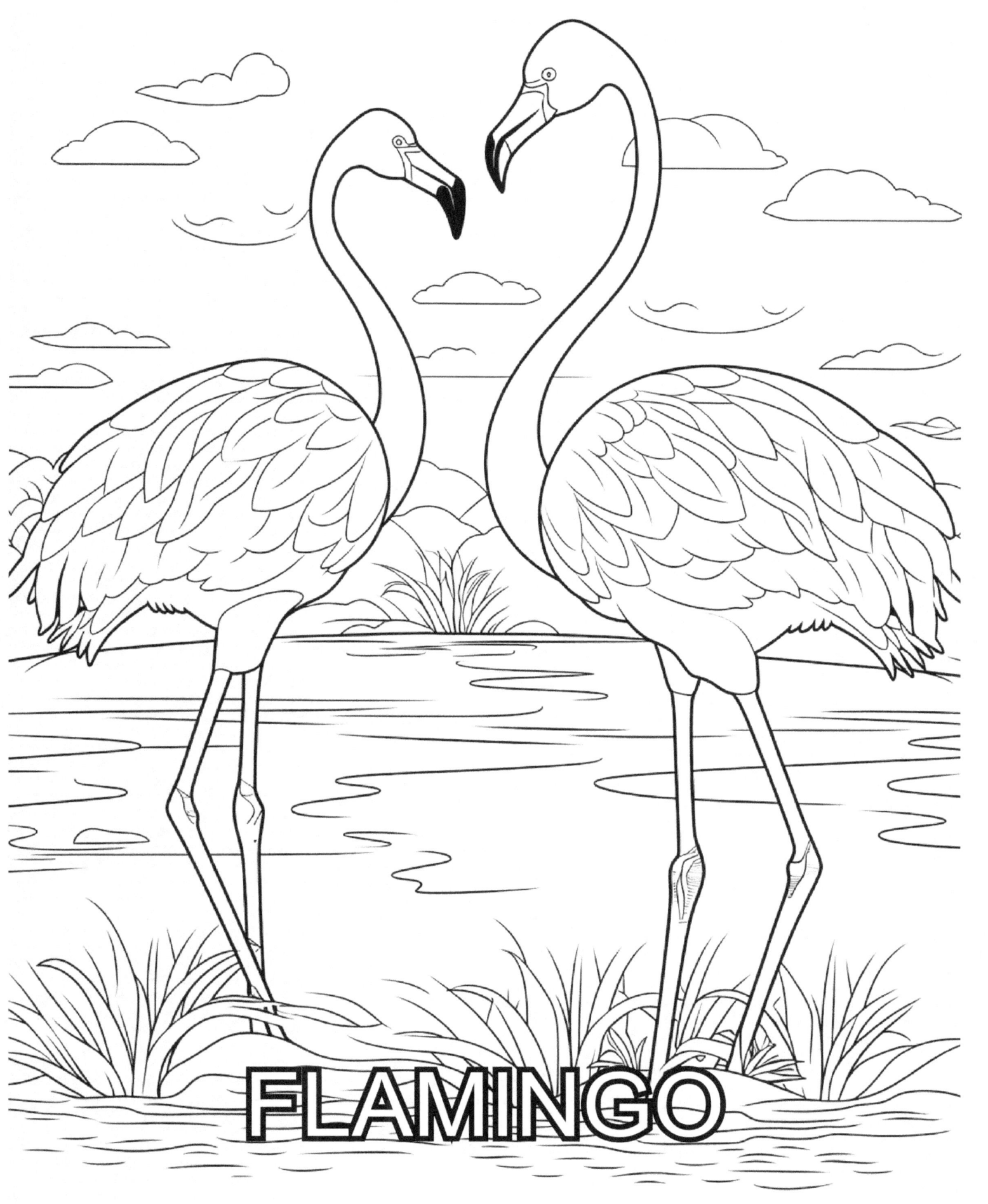

FLAMINGO

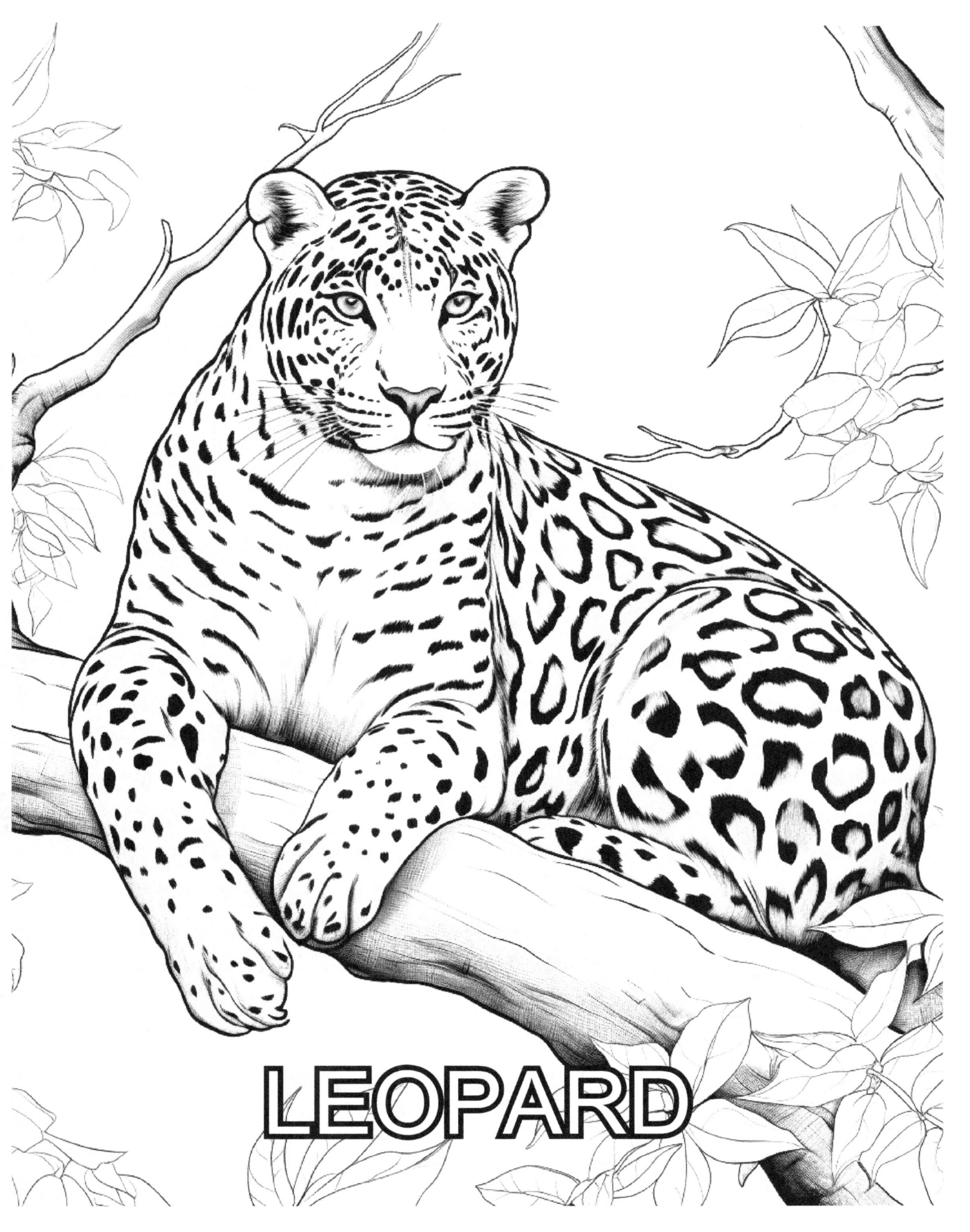

LEOPARD

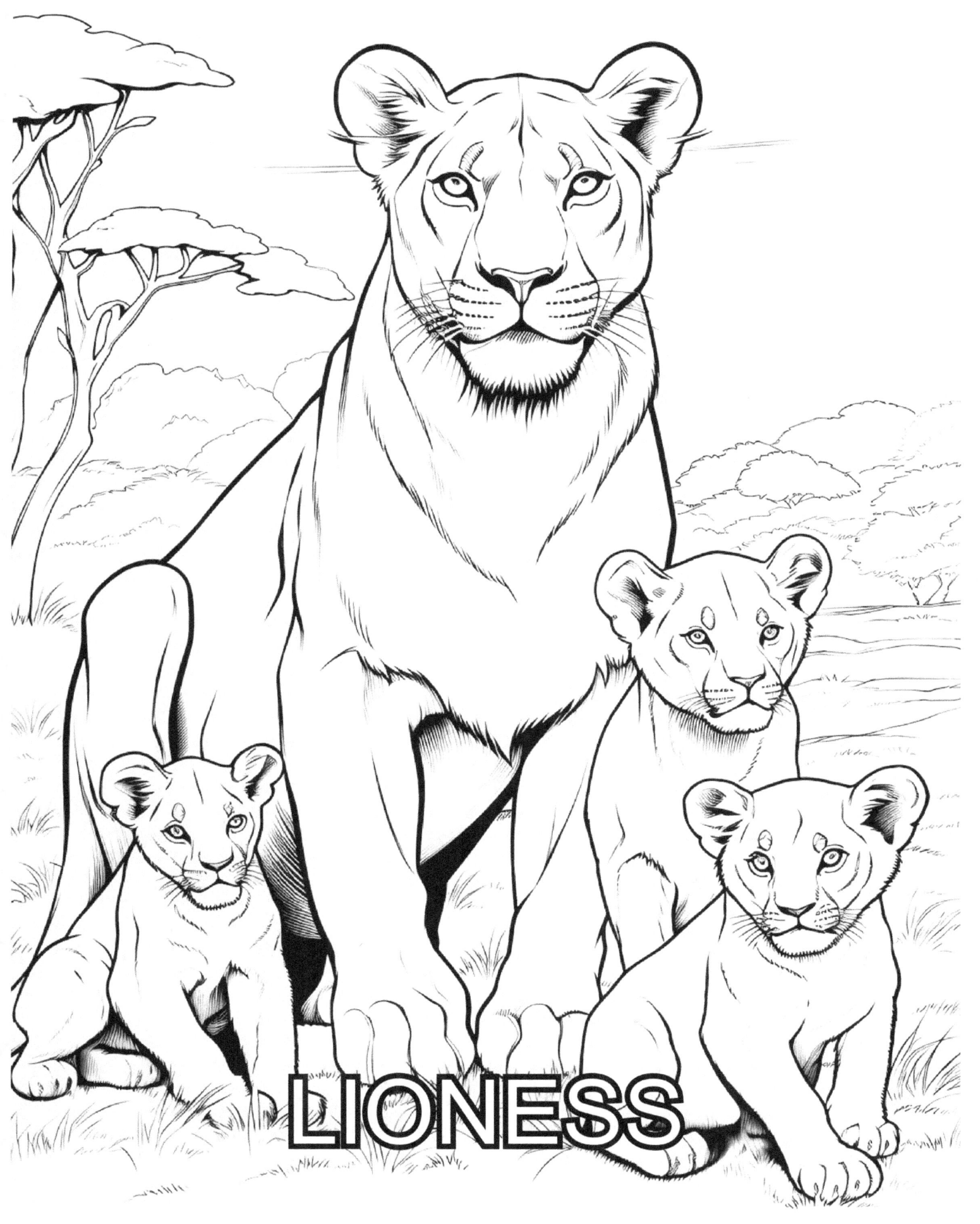

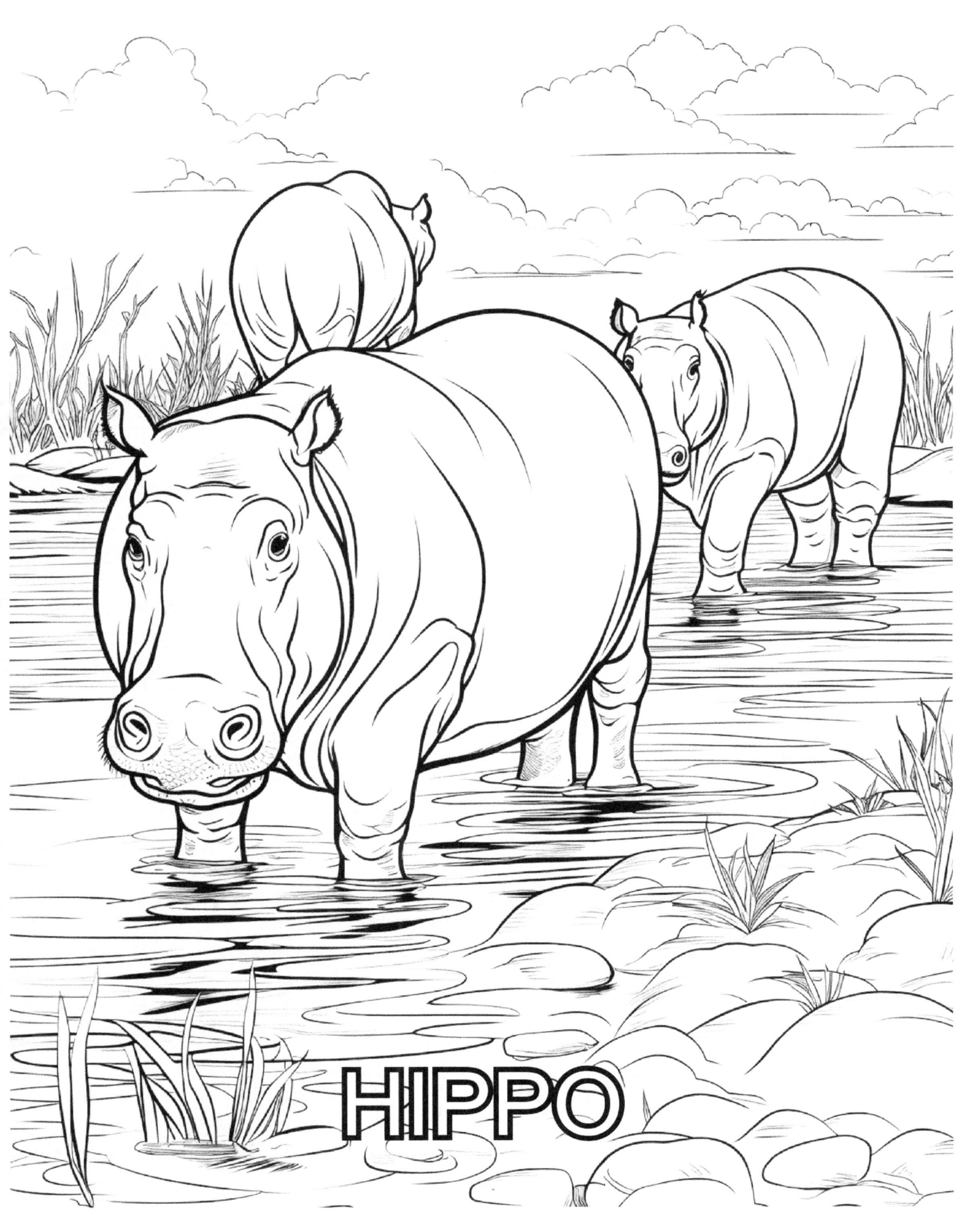

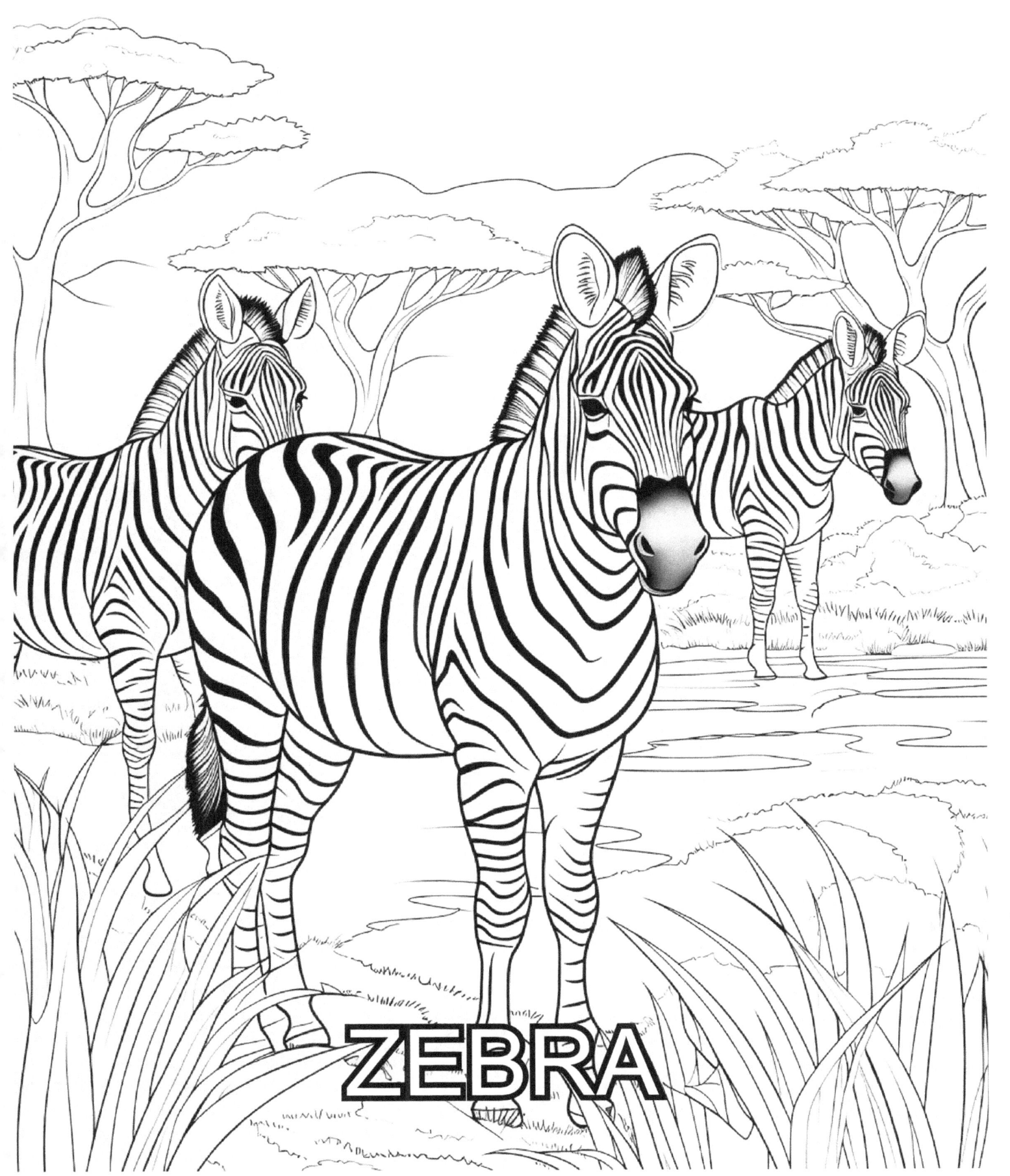

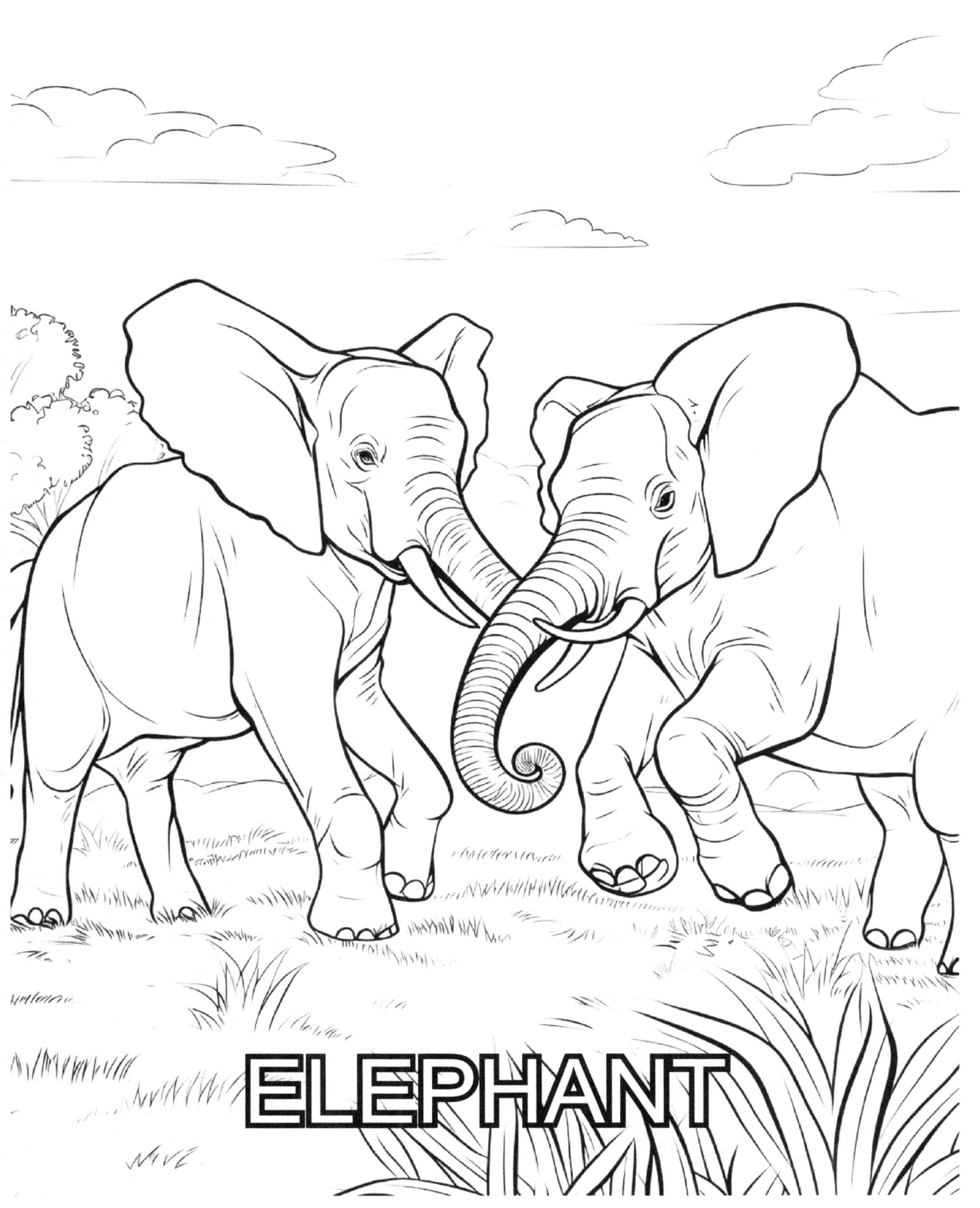

ELEPHANT

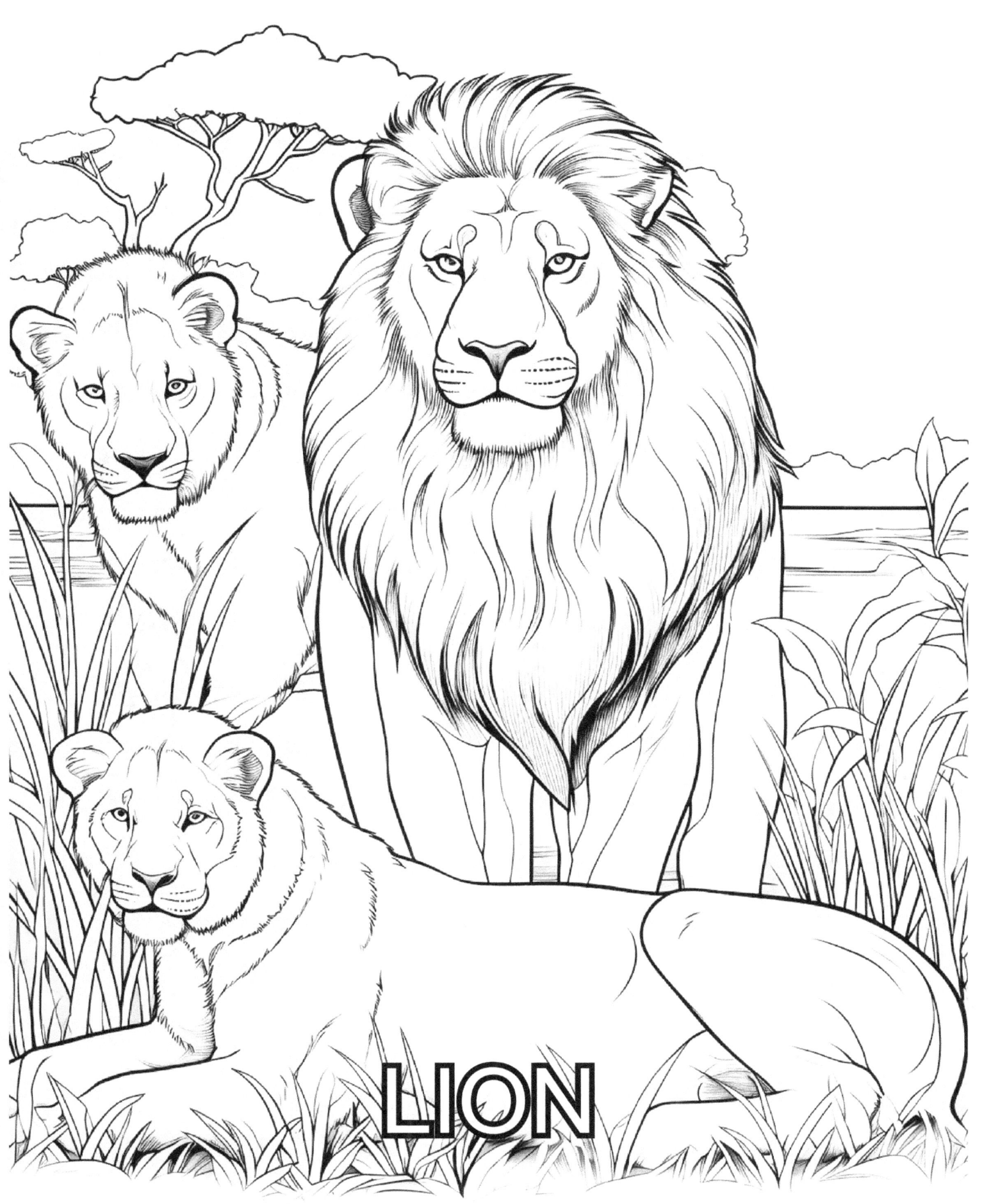

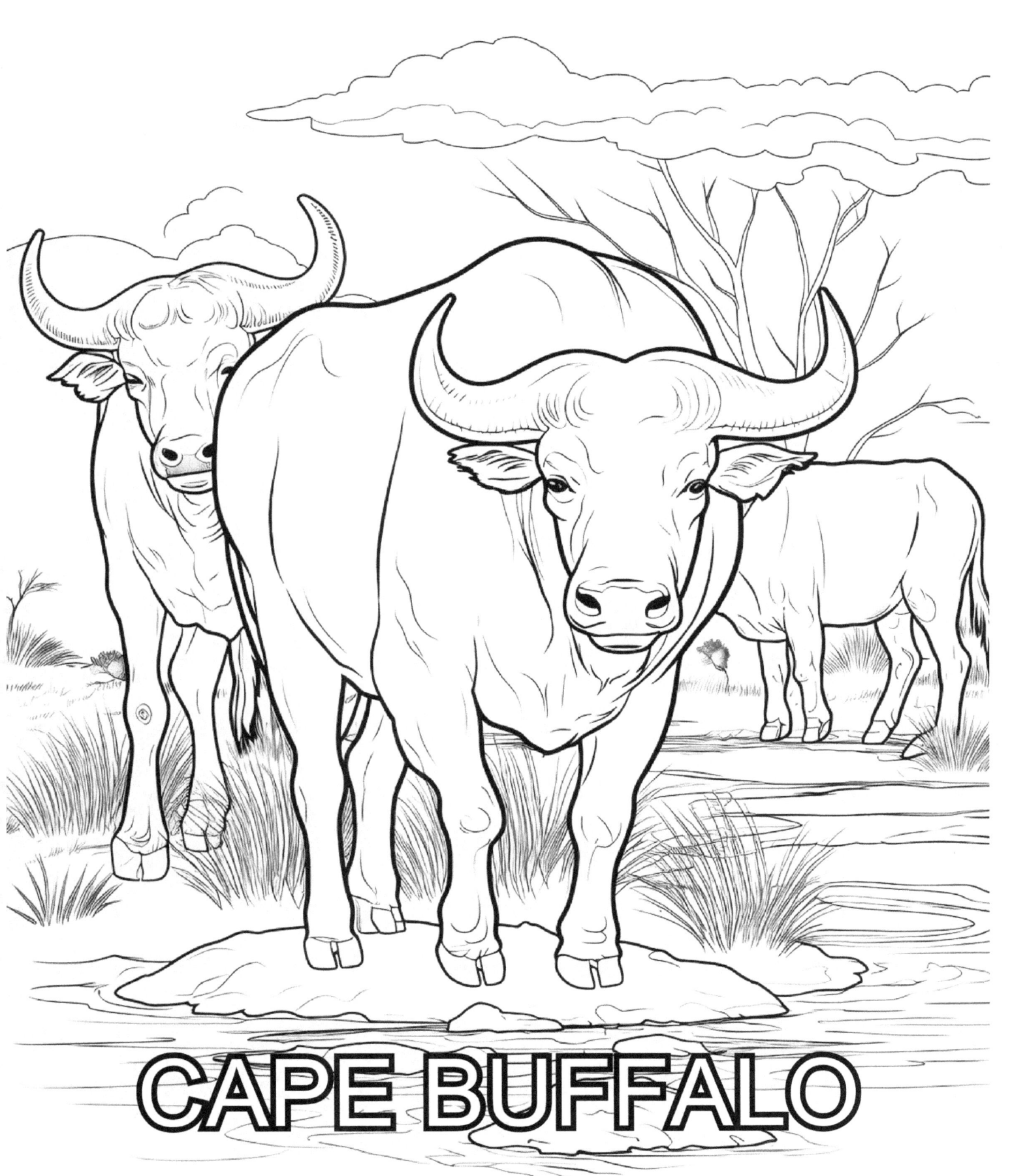

CAPE BUFFALO

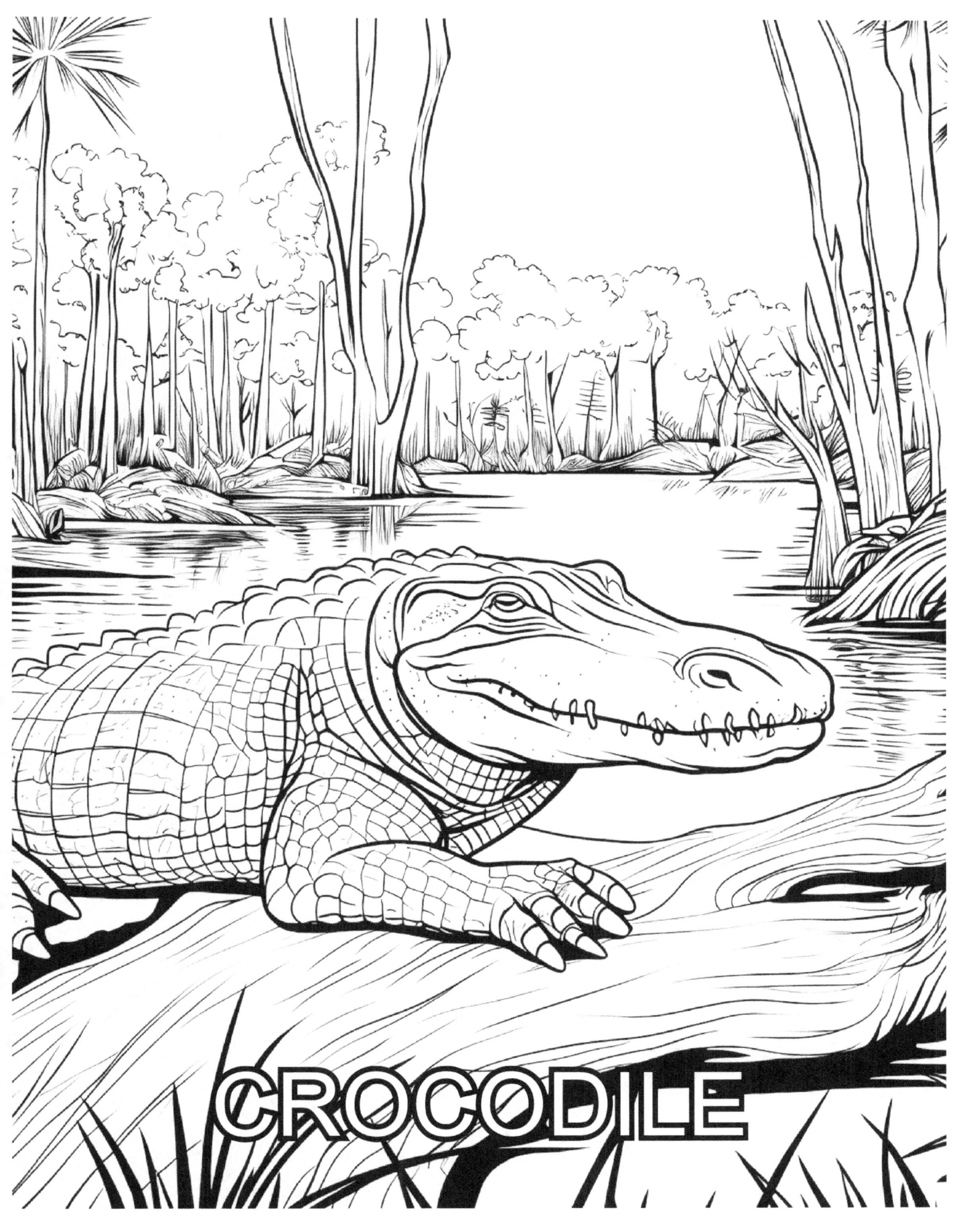

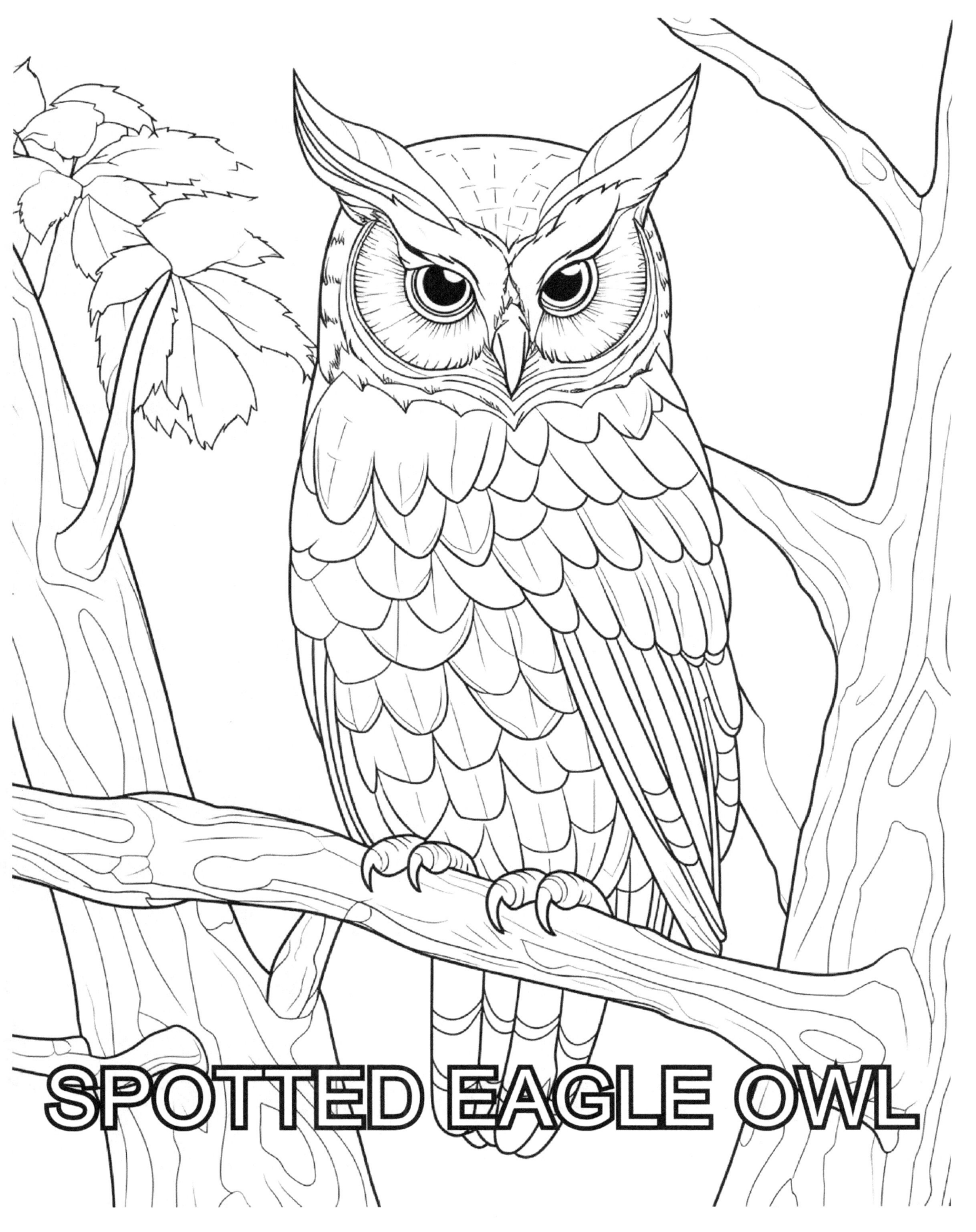

SPOTTED EAGLE OWL

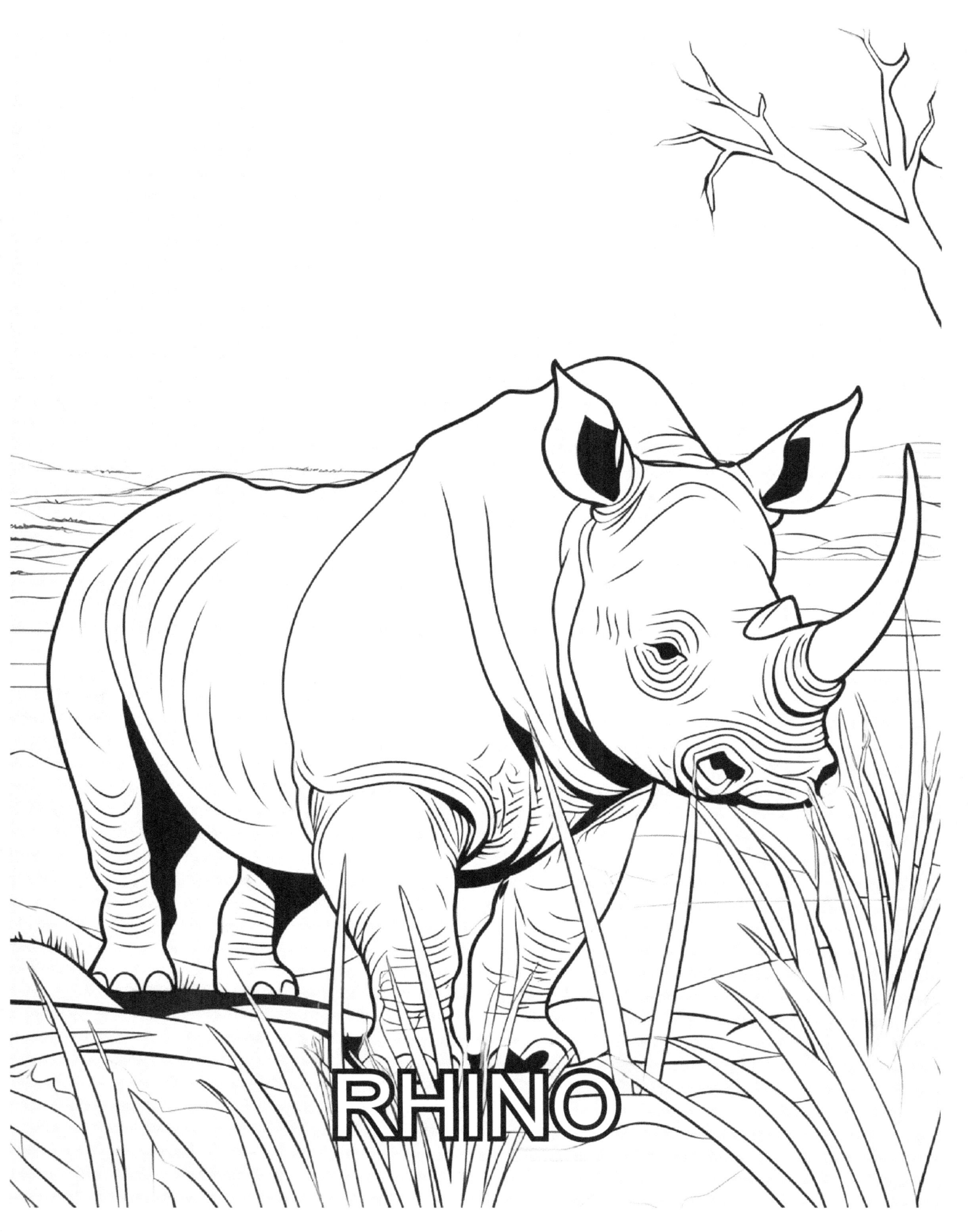

RHINO

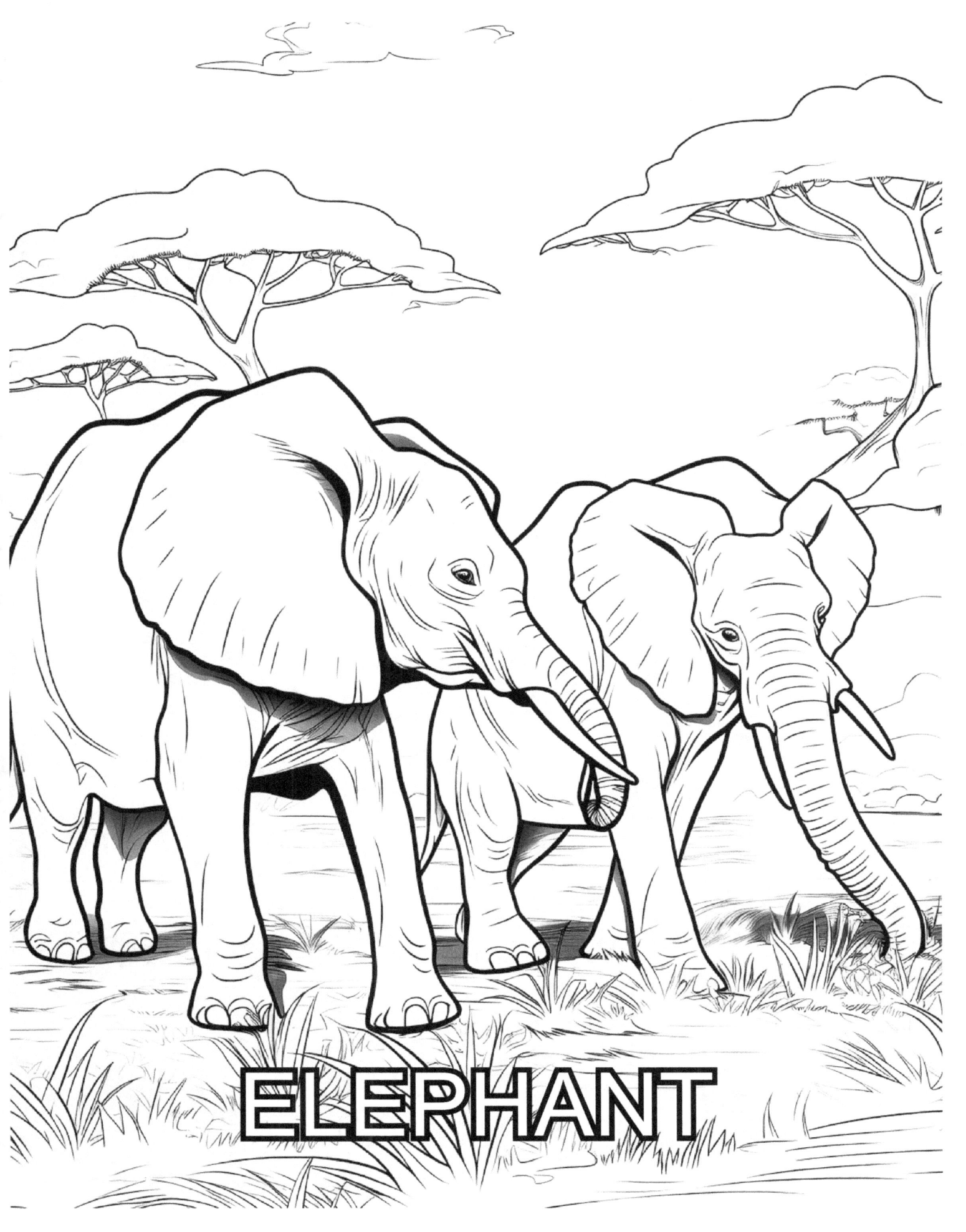

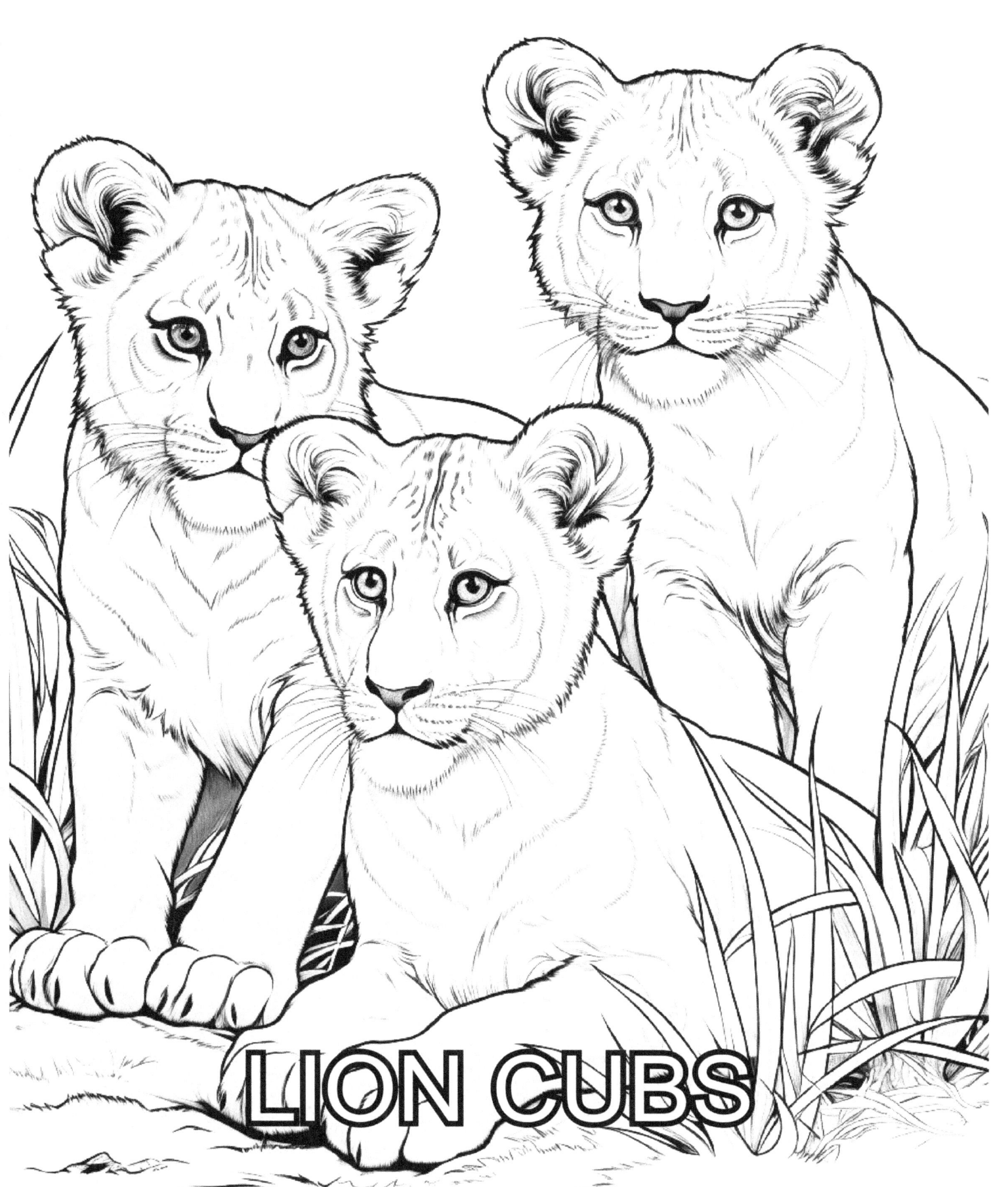

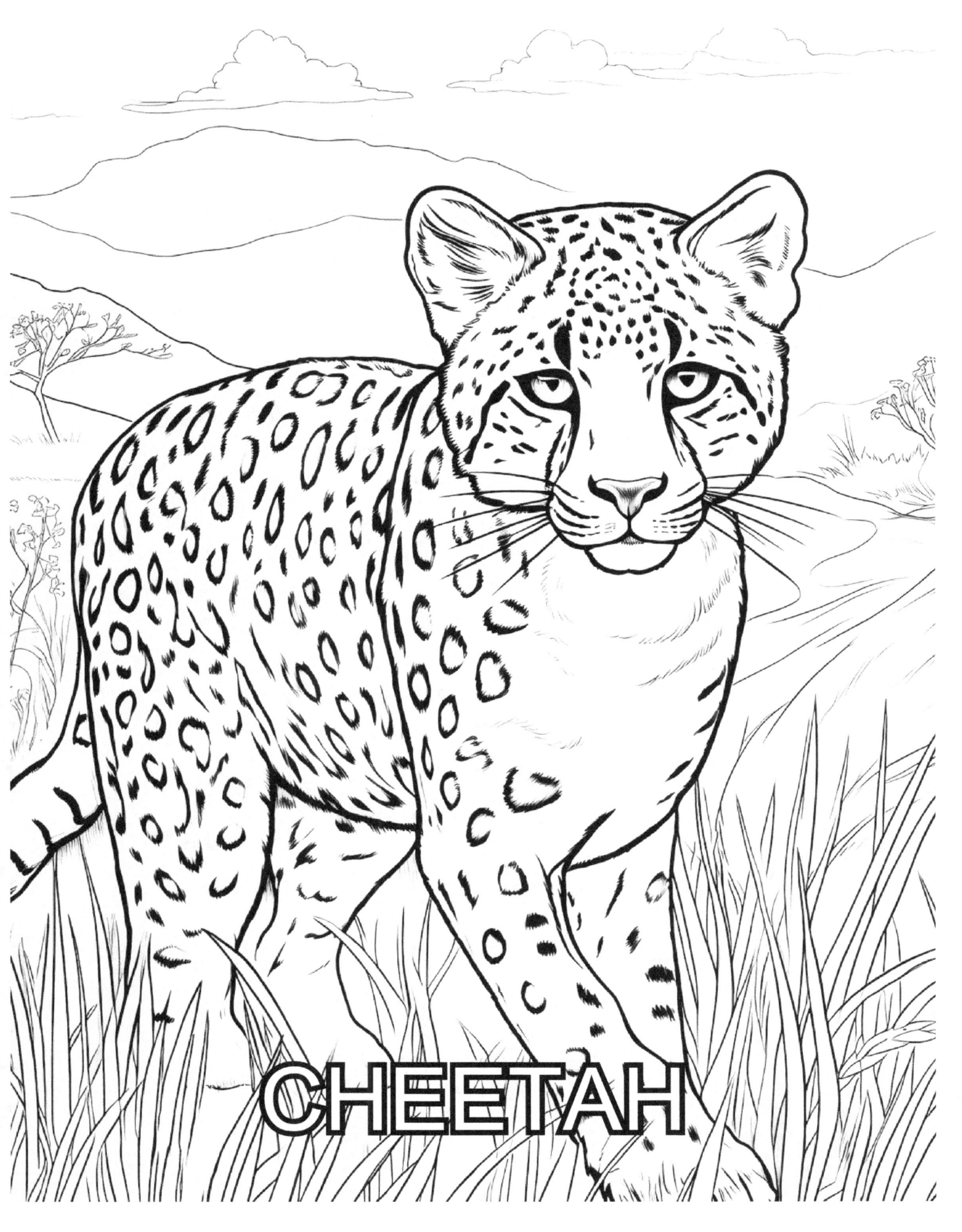

CHEETAH

# Your feedback is greatly appreciated!

It's through your feedback, support and reviews that we're able to create the best books possible and serve more people.

We would be extremely grateful if you could take just 60 seconds to kindly leave an honest review of the book on Amazon. Please share your feedback and thoughts for others to see.

To do so, simply find the book on Amazon's website (or wherever you purchased the book from) and locate the section to leave a review. Select a star rating and write a couple of sentences.

That's it! Thank you so much for your support.

## Review this product

Share your thoughts with other customers

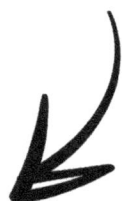

Write a customer review

Or just scan here and leave a review

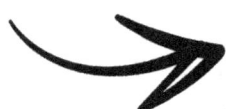